The People and the Mob

The People and the Mob

THE IDEOLOGY OF CIVIL CONFLICT
IN MODERN EUROPE

Peter Hayes

Westport, Connecticut
London

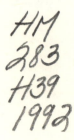

Library of Congress Cataloging-in-Publication Data

Hayes, Peter.
    The people and the mob : the ideology of civil conflict in modern
Europe / Peter Hayes.
      p. cm.
    Includes bibliographical references and index.
    ISBN 0-275-94336-4
    1. Collective behavior—History. 2. Mobs—Europe—History.
3. Crowds—Europe—History. 4. Fascism—Europe—History.
5. Ideology—History. 6. Social conflict—Europe—History.
I. Title.
HM283.H39 1992
302.3'3—dc20   92–9826

British Library Cataloguing in Publication Data is available.

Library of Congress Catalog Card Number: 92–9826
ISBN: 0–275–94336–4

First published in 1992

Praeger Publishers, 88 Post Road West, Westport, CT 06881
An imprint of Greenwood Publishing Group, Inc.

Printed in the United States of America

The paper used in this book complies with the Permanent
Paper Standard issued by the National Information Standards
Organization (Z39.48—1984).

10 9 8 7 6 5 4 3 2 1

To Mary

Contents

Figures

Acknowledgments

I would like to thank Marvin Weinbaum, Jeff Cohen, and Belden Fields of the University of Illinois for the useful and constructive criticisms they provided on this work. I would also like to thank another member of the political science faculty at Illinois, Peter Nardulli, for facilitating the year I spent in Britain.

It was during my time in Britain that I conducted most of the interviews on the 1984–85 British miners' strike cited in Chapter 6. This was the most enjoyable part of my research, largely because of the friendly reception and generous assistance I received from people who had been involved in the dispute. Some of them spoke to me briefly but with feeling; others gave me many hours of their time. I would first like to thank Peggy Kahn and Vic Allen, two academics who have had connections with the National Union of Mineworkers (NUM), for discussing the strike with me. I am particularly grateful to Professor Kahn for her hospitality and for making available her collection of published material on the strike. I would also like to thank members of the NUM, the Union of Democratic Mineworkers (UDM), and others associated with the strike who agreed to speak with me. Several of these people spoke on the condition of anonymity. However, I am able to mention Roy Bentley, Allen Burely, Colin Brady, Peter Coxhill, Mrs. Coxhill, Loo Curtis, William Gaskell, Allen Kirby, Peter Naylor, Mick Oliver, Al Payne, David Prendergast, Ralph Pywell, John Scott, Fred Stansborough, Kevin Ward, Paul Whetton, and Paul Whitehead. The strike is a subject about which people have strong views, and I am sorry if my interpretation of it appears inaccurate or offensive to any of those I interviewed.

I would like to thank Raymond Plant for facilitating access to Southampton University Library. I am also very grateful to July Crawley, who was a great help at Exeter University Library.

My parents, Mike and Mary, were very supportive of me throughout the period in which I worked on the book. I would also like to thank two of my uncles, Paul and Peter, and my grandma, Ethel, for the very considerable assistance that they have given to me.

Finally, I would like to thank my wife, Mary, for all of the help and encouragement she has given to me.

Introduction

The anti-democrats and reactionaries of eighteenth- and nineteenth-century Europe disparaged the bulk of the population, using terms such as "rabble," "swinish multitude," and "herd."[1] A particularly common term was the "mob," an abbreviation of the Latin *mobile vulgus,* or turbulent common people. A few radical democrats and supporters of the French Revolution, such as Jean-Jacques Rousseau and Thomas Paine, redefined the majority of society positively, not as the mob but as "the people." Now, 200 years later, the ideals of democracy are universally acknowledged in one form or another. Exponents of contemporary political ideologies in Europe, however else they may differ, are similar in their claims to being democrats.

As democratic ideology has taken hold in Europe, so "the people" has displaced pejorative appellations for the majority of the population such as the "mob." But despite the increasing ubiquity of democratic norms, the mob has remained a part of political rhetoric. The meaning behind the term, however, has shifted in two ways. First, the mob has come to be used in a way that complements rather than contradicts the idea of the people. It is no longer used to refer to the majority of society, but rather to a minority. Second, the mob is no longer seen as being composed of an integral constituent of society, the common people, whose fault lies in perpetrating acts of disorder. Instead, the very existence of the mob as a social category is seen as useless or malign. It is described as scum or sediment that has separated itself from mainstream society. Its members are not of society; they are the enemies within.

This revised idea of the mob was not invented in the eighteenth century. Its earliest appearance in European political thought goes back to Plato's description of parasitic "drones" in a democracy.[2] Plato wrote that in contrast to "the people," whose desires were necessary and "productive because they're useful for production," drones had "a mob of useless desires."[3] These drones also associated with slaves and mercenary foreigners, the "riffraff washed in by every sea," and maliciously incited the people against the rich.[4] Plato concluded that drones could not be incorporated into a healthy political body, but only excised from it: They "agitate the whole regime like bile and phlegm in the body, and a good doctor and lawgiver must take precautions like a wise beekeeper preferably to prevent them from hatching, or if they do, to have both them and their cells cut out of the hive."[5] A similar picture of a wicked, unproductive, useless group that posed a threat both in itself and in its agitation of the industrious majority can be discerned in late medieval laws against vagabondage.[6] However, it has been in the last 200 years, from the French Revolution to the current revolutions in Eastern Europe, the age of mass politics, that the mob has assumed a particular ideological significance.

The use of a dichotomy between the people and the mob by those with an ideological agenda has a certain logic to it across a wide range of historical circumstances. In its simplest form, this logic dictates that "the people" is used to refer to supporters and "the mob" to opponents, even though each group might in fact have a similar social composition. Thus, an editorial from 1831 points out: "At a Reform Meeting, the populace, consist of whom it may, are called 'the people'; but if riot ensues, the very same personages are then designated a *mob*."[7] Mark Harrison, who discovered this passage, has argued that in early nineteenth-century England, the term "the mob" was used in place of "people" when crowds become violent or attacked property. This selective use of people and mob aptly summarizes the rhetoric of those concerned to defend order or the status quo in Europe. However, the concept of the mob has not been the preserve of moderates, conservatives, and reactionaries, but rather has, like that of the people, been a useful component of ideologies across the political spectrum.

The use of the people–mob dichotomy by populist and avowedly radical ideologues and commentators has a more ambiguous relationship to violence and disorder than when it is used by defenders of the establishment. One of the main tasks of this work is to specify the forms that this ambiguous relationship has taken. Therefore, I have focused on the use of the distinction between the people and the mob in ideologies that have challenged the status quo, including fascism, corporatism, socialism, and nationalism. Particular attention has been given to the place of the mob in Marx's writings. This, I hope, will serve to refute the assumption that Marx's class theory is inimical to the division of society into people and mob and that Marxist ideology is immune to the political pressures to adopt such a classification.

The book is divided into two parts. The first five chapters show how the idea of the mob has been incorporated into modern political ideologies by establishing how it has been connected to the idea of the people, by tracing some of the intellectual developments and adaptations that have been made to these two concepts over the last 200 years and by examining the ideological uses to which they have been put. In this part of the work, I describe how "mob" and "people" have become apparently complementary rather than overtly contradictory terms, in a way that has allowed various ideologies to succeed in gaining widespread support. Chapter 1 provides an overview of this process in Europe after the French Revolution. This chapter also introduces a subject pursued throughout the book: the way in which various depictions of the mob and the people have been influenced by the work ethic. Chapter 2 begins to examine the mob in Marx's thought by considering how he linked his analysis of the role played by the lumpenproletariat in the French coup d'état of 1851 to his dialectical theory of revolution. Chapter 3 considers Marx's class analysis of events in France in general, including the February Revolution and June Insurrection of 1848 and the Paris Commune of 1871. This chapter also has a detailed discussion of ideological flexibility and adaptation. Chapter 4 takes up the concept of ideological flexibility in an analysis of the relationship between crowd theory and fascism. It argues that fascist ideology exploited the ambiguous identification of mass groups as both the mob and the people found in crowd theory. Chapter 5 considers how the concept of the mob and the people informed fascist doctrines of corporatism between the wars and how this distinguishes fascist from democratic forms of corporatism. This chapter concludes with a general discussion of the ideological rationale for distinguishing between the people and the mob.

Part II of the work examines two cases that illustrate the problematic relationship between ideologies that make use of the distinction between the people and the mob and democracy. The first case, presented in Chapter 6, looks at the ideological debate that occurred during 1984–85 miners' strike in Britain. Union activists in the strike faced a dilemma: Given the democratic norms held by themselves and by other union members in Britain from which they sought support, it was both doctrinally and practically necessary to claim that the majority was on their side during the strike. However, the strike had not been preceded by a national ballot, and a significant section of the miners refused to stop work. The response of strike activists was, first, to describe the working miners as scabs, and, second, to develop a revised (and somewhat suspect) idea of union democracy. The second case, presented in Chapter 7, looks at the events in progress in Eastern Europe. This final chapter examines the dilemmas involved in attempting to develop a pluralist democracy in societies where political success depends on appealing to the people.

The examination of the people and the mob as ideological concepts is quite distinct from their use in social analysis. Perhaps the best-known analytic use of such a distinction is found in the first ten chapters of Hannah Arendt's *The Origins of Totalitarianism.*[8] Arendt explained her distinction between these groups under the subheading, "The People and the Mob": "The mob is primarily a group in which the residue of all classes are represented. This makes it so easy to mistake the mob for the people, which also comprises all strata of society."[9] However, Arendt argued, unlike the people, the mob was not involved in production, and while this may have been involuntary, members of the mob could also be distinguished from the people by their "negative . . . decision against [joining] the workers' movements."[10]

The Origins is instructive not because of its historical contentions, which are disputed, but rather because it shows how the analytic distinction between the people and the mob can be used for ideological purposes. In Arendt's case, the ideological objective is to exonerate the working class from involvement in anti-Semitism and imperialism. She achieves this aim in two ways. The first is simply to attribute anti-Semitic outrages and imperialist expansion to the mob.[11] The second method, used to distance the working class from anti-Semitism, is somewhat more convoluted. It proceeds in four steps. First, Arendt extends the meaning of the mob to include the unproductive rich. (This step is typical of many of the ideologies that will be examined.) Second, she identifies financiers as exemplifying this unproductive group.[12] Third, she associates financiers with Jews.[13] Fourth, she identifies mass-based hostility to this wealthy mob with the petit bourgeoisie. Thus, Arendt described how during the nineteenth century:

To the small shopkeeper the banker appeared to be the same kind of exploiter as the owner of a big industrial enterprise was to the worker. But while the European workers, from their own experience, and a Marxist education in economics, knew that the capitalist filled the double function of exploiting them and giving them the opportunity to produce, the small shopkeeper had found nobody to enlighten him about his social and economic destiny. His predicament was even worse than the worker's and on the basis of his experience he considered the banker a parasite and usurer whom he had to make his silent partner, even though this banker, in contrast to the manufacturer, had nothing whatsoever to do with his business. It is not difficult to comprehend that a man who put his money solely and directly to the use of begetting more money can be hated more bitterly than the one who gets his profit through a lengthy and involved process of production.[14]

My argument diverges from Arendt's analysis in this passage in three areas. First, differences between financiers and manufacturers are not in fact determined by their productivity or lack of productivity. Distinctions between these groups based on productivity are ideologically but not analytically significant. Second, as will be seen in Chapter 3, Arendt's emphasis on the involvement of employers in the productive process can indeed be said to be a "Marxist" perspective in cases where Marxists have appealed for support from property-owning classes. However, Marxism's distinct appeal to the working class—and Marxism had only a limited impact on Europe's working class in the nineteenth century[15]—was its suggestion that workers replaced the "opportunity to produce" for manufacturers with the opportunity to produce for themselves. This aspect of Marxism generally condemned employers as parasites in the same way that others condemned bankers. Third, Arendt's identification of the direct relationship between the petit bourgeoisie and bankers is interesting in that it might help explain why this class had a particular propensity to be opposed to financiers or anti-Semitic. However, the corporatist, nationalist, and fascist ideologies that adopted these views also attributed the antagonism between capital and labor to the malign influence of bankers. These forms of ideology gained significant working-class support, particularly during the interwar period.

Arendt's argument that the working class was involved neither in imperialism nor in anti-Semitism is representative of a broader intellectual tendency to disassociate the working class from undesirable forms of political activity. In later chapters, it will be seen that this type of perspective has encouraged the adoption of the mob as an explanation of convenience by the left. In the opening chapter, however, the tendency to idealize the working class is criticized not for promoting the use of the mob, but for failing to acknowledge the significant ideological appeal of the term as it was used in political rhetoric from the late eighteenth to the later nineteenth century.

NOTES

1. In French, these terms included *populace, canaille, tourbe*; in German, *Pöbel*.

2. Plato, *The Republic*, trans. Raymond Larson (Arlington Heights, Il.: Harlan Davidson, 1979), pp. 559–69.

3. Ibid., pp. 559c, 560d. The word here translated as "mob" is *plethos*, which means mass or multitude. Larson's translation, however, correctly conveys the evaluative import of the term in this context.

4. Ibid., pp. 569a, 565b-c.

5. Ibid., pp. 564b-c.

6. See A. L. Beier, *Masterless Men: The Vagrancy Problem in England 1560–1640* (London: Methuen, 1985), pp. 4, 12, 15; Cesare Lombroso, *Crime, Its Causes and Remedies*, trans. Henry P. Horton (Boston: Little Brown, 1911), p. 68n; Karl Marx, *Capital* (Chicago: Charles Kerr, 1912), Vol. 1, pp. 806–8.

7. *Felix Farley's Bristol Journal*, 12 November 1831, cited in Mark Harrison, *Crowds and History: Mass Phenomena in English Towns, 1790–1835* (Cambridge: Cambridge University Press, 1988), p. 189.

8. Hannah Arendt, *The Origins of Totalitarianism*, 3rd ed. (New York: Harcourt, Brace and World, 1966), pp. 3–340. Arendt more or less abandoned the people and the mob in her concluding analysis of totalitarianism by claiming that the rise of the masses made these social categories irrelevant. This shift paved the way for her very different view of productivity in modern society in *The Human Condition* (Chicago: University of Chicago Press, 1958).

9. Arendt, *The Origins*, p. 107.

10. Ibid., p. 189.

11. Ibid., pp. 106–17, 185–221.

12. Ibid., pp. 147–55.

13. Ibid., pp. 37, 198–203.

14. Ibid., p. 37.

15. See Dick Geary, *European Labour Protest 1848–1939* (London: Croom Helm, 1981).

PART I

IDEOLOGY

CHAPTER 1

The Ideological Functions
of the Mob

The mob has often been described as rising from darkness and descending again to haunts unknown. Alphonse de Lamartine described the Paris insurgents of June 1848 as:

> A mass of about twenty thousand vagrants . . . living unseen in tranquil times, coming from the shade, and covering the streets, in days of civil commotion. A signal from the chief, a nocturnal appeal from their accomplices, suffice to rally them in a moment.[1]

"Never had any been seen like them in open day. . . . Where do they come from? Who has brought them out of their obscure hiding places?" asked Baron de Besenval of the French revolutionaries.[2]

"The passive protestors . . . were fast swelling their ranks with undesirable recruits; ill conditioned ruffians drawn from . . . dark courts, blind alleys and unsavoury night cellars," wrote J. P. de Castro of the participants in the Gordon riots.[3] The imagery is apt because the social composition of the protesters is conjured up almost from nowhere. Recent historical investigations into these events, as well as other revolutions and riots attributed to the mob, have found the participants to be workers or petit bourgeois. In no case, however, has the social group identified with the mob accounted for more than an insignificant number of those involved.[4]

In light of these studies, it might be concluded that the mob has little theoretical value in explanations of political conflict, but this would be to ignore the concept's function as an element of ideology. The use of the mob is not restricted to explanation per se but may also serve the ideological purpose of protecting certain beliefs or furthering certain objectives. Furthermore, the identification of groups engaged in mass conflict as the mob is not something that is confined to historians such as de Castro; it has also been done by those directly affected by or actively involved in the conflict, such as Besenval, commander of the King's troops in Paris at the outset of the French Revolution, and Lamartine, a leading member of the Second Republic. In other words, the mob is related to the beliefs and objectives of participants in mass conflict as well as to later ideological debates over the interpretation of such conflict. Examining the ideological functions of the mob, therefore, shifts the assessment of the concept's significance away from the question of who has been involved in mass conflict. Instead, it asks why those involved in political conflict have identified their adversaries as the mob.

MEANINGS OF THE "MOB"

The mob is typically depicted as a being composed of beggars, vagabonds, and criminals. These occupations, however, do not define the mob so much as epitomize the characteristics associated with a much broader social group. Hippolyte Taine, for example, described the mob in the French Revolution as including

> "Idlers, libertines, professional gamblers," kept-*sigisbes*, intriguers, parasites, and adventurers, elbow men with branded shoulders, the veterans of vice and crime, "the scrapegraces of the . . . galleys," . . . the rabble of the town, . . . peasants hating the *octroi*, vagabonds, smugglers, fugitives from justice, vagrant foreigners, marauders and malefactors.[5]

In a similar vein, Karl Marx described the Parisian supporters of Louis Napoleon as

> decayed *roues* with dubious means of subsistence and of dubious

origin, . . . ruined and adventurous offshoots of the bourgeoisie, . . . vagabonds, discharged soldiers, discharged jailbirds, escaped galley slaves,
rogues, mountebanks, *lazzaroni*, pickpockets, tricksters, gamblers, *ma-
quereaus*, brothel keepers, porters, *literati*, organ-grinders, rag-pickers,
knifegrinders, tinkers, beggars.[6]

The picture of the mob drawn in such descriptions is of an immoral,
impoverished, and marginal social group. Its members lie beyond the
bounds of mainstream society because they have no regular occupation,
are unwilling to engage in work, and produce nothing. Their political
actions are illegitimate, and they are often said to have been bribed to
undertake them. Those whose occupations are listed above do not always
share in all of these characteristics. They do, however, cluster around
them in a way that makes the overall import of the depictions clear: The
mob is the combination, for wicked purposes, of those who are poor and
unproductive, a combination that constitutes a political threat despite the
marginal social status of its members.

It is certainly possible to see why such a mob might be the object
of political opposition, including mass opposition, as its qualities are
those of a feared and hated outgroup. But if the mob is to be understood
as anything more than a convenient scapegoat, it must be asked (1)
why these particular qualities have been used to depict it; and (2) what
principles tie them together. To answer these questions, it is necessary to
examine the beliefs and objectives of those who depicted their opponents
as the mob.

This chapter will begin this investigation by focusing on Europe,
particularly England and France, from around the time of the French
Revolution until the late nineteenth century. During this time, the mob,
that is, an unproductive, immoral, minority group, typified the hostile
portrayal of those involved in mass action. The end of this period,
however, is bounded by three intellectual developments that made the
idea of the mob considerably more complex (they will be discussed
in detail in Chapter 4). One of these developments was the idea of
national energy, an *élan vital*, that could be expressed through mass
violence. Two other ideas of great significance were social Darwinism
and crowd theory.

Although Darwin revolutionized biological classification, social Darwinists did not reclassify the established boundaries of the mob. Their
concept of a degenerate class[7] identified a group whose characteristics
and social composition were very similar to earlier depictions of the

mob. Social Darwinists did, however, adapt this classification by adding a distinctive explanation of why the mob held dangerous and criminal propensities. Where such propensities had previously been attributed to the environmental or moral determinants of mob behavior,[8] social Darwinists identified inherent traits and racial characteristics.[9]

The third development occurred with the interest generated in crowd behavior by the work of Gustave Le Bon and others.[10] Although crowd theorists sometimes drew on the existing classification of the mob as an outcast social group, they simultaneously undermined it by radically reinterpreting the basis of mob activity. Before the appearance of crowd theory, mob action was generally seen as the aggregate expression of the character and objectives of the individuals who composed the mob. Crowd theorists, however, stressed the distinction between individual behavior and the behavior of crowd members, and thus separated the question of the motives, propensities, and aims of social groups prior to their forming a crowd from their behavior in a crowd.

It is not just in the twentieth century that the concept of the mob has changed. Until the late 1700s, the mob was typically depicted not as a wicked, unproductive minority but rather as the majority of the population. This depiction drew on the classical picture of the mob as the *mobile vulgus*, the unstable common people.

William Watson, for example, described how the authority of church and state was challenged by the Jesuit plot

> to make it seeme meet to the ignorant multitude & afterwards to others (for note this, that popularitie is the rouer they aim at in all their proceedings, the *mobile vulgus* being ever wavering and readiest to run upon every change) that the whole Cleargie . . . should be subject to them.[11]

It can be seen from this passage that the *mobile vulgus* is conceptually rather than simply etymologically related to the later depiction of the mob; the idea of a threatening combination of the poor is present in both cases. In addition, the *mobile vulgus*, like the mob, is seen as a marginal group in the sense that it is without a legitimate claim to involvement in political or social affairs.[12] But whether the concept of the *mobile vulgus* possesses the other qualities associated with the concept of the mob is rather more ambiguous. Watson indicted the Jesuits as agitators who manipulated the multitude, but the masses themselves are seen as being moved at random, without purposes of their own. There is therefore no clear indication that the *mobile vulgus* is immoral. Furthermore, Watson suggests that the *mobile vulgus* is neither unproductive nor a minority. Why then were these characteristics of the mob adopted in later explanations of hostile mass action? To answer this question, it is helpful to investigate the range of ideologies that were developing in the eighteenth and nineteenth centuries.

CONSERVATISM AND RADICALISM

Much of the political thought of the late eighteenth and early nineteenth century can be located on a continuum between the conservative defense of established elites at one end and middle class radicalism at the other. The explanation of hostile mass action as coming from the *mobile vulgus* is most closely associated with the conservative end of this spectrum.[13] However, where such a doctrine includes a theory of the organic state, certain difficulties can be seen to arise in reconciling belief in such a theory with the attribution of mass opposition to the *mobile vulgus*. In order to preserve an organic view of the state, those who threaten its order may be described as foreign to the social body or as a cancer upon it. Such a malignant group, however, can hardly be equated with the majority of a society without calling the whole organic analogy into question. At the very least, it would seem that a threat coming from the majority would require the identification of an honest mistake. Thus, Edmund Burke argued that "the people have no interest in disorder. When they do wrong, it is their error, and not their crime."[14]

Alternatively, a threatening majority could be seen to contain an evil minority who acted to corrupt the whole. This type of explanation was condemned by William Cobbett: "They can find no *agitators*. It is a movement of the *people's own*."[15]

Conservatives also faced a second difficulty if they described the majority as the *mobile vulgus*. This problem was of a practical rather than a theoretical nature, a dilemma of circumstances rather than belief. In one sense, for conservatives to equate the bulk of the population with the *mobile vulgus* was not a mistaken prejudice; it correctly denoted the potential threat of the masses to the status quo. Yet to openly depict mass groups in such a way might in itself generate or exacerbate such a threat. This dilemma was exemplified by the response to Burke's description of "a swinish multitude," which, taken to imply "that swinishness was the inherent character of the multitude . . . was the principal theme of popular demonstrations against his book."[16] The same dilemma can be seen just before the Gordon riots. When a mass of angry Protestants converged on Parliament, Lord George Gordon left the debate over Catholic rights on the floor of the House to inform them that "Lord North calls you a mob."[17]

In a discussion on wealth and poverty in civil society, G. W. F. Hegel contended that a certain type of mass threat to the political and social order originated, by definition, from a lazy, marginal, minority social group. His analysis suggested how conservatives could resolve the difficulties of interpreting mass opposition to the status quo by attributing it to the unproductive mob rather than by characterizing the general mass of the poor as the *mobile vulgus*. Hegel wrote:

> Poverty in itself does not make men into a rabble; a rabble is created only when there is joined to poverty a disposition of mind, an inner indignation against the rich, against society, against the government, &c. Another consequence of this attitude is that through their dependence on chance men become frivolous and idle, like the Neapolitan *lazzaroni* for example. In this way is born in the rabble the evil of lacking self-respect enough to secure subsistence by its own labour and yet at the same time of claiming to receive subsistence as its right.[18]

The advantages of this argument were, first, that it was consistent with an organic theory of class relations and, second, that while it condemned a part of the poor, did so in a way which did not antagonize the majority of the population with the "self-respect" to work. At the same time, because the definition of those who threatened the established order was a false one, the argument remained, objectively, an expression of hostility to demands emanating from working groups among the masses.[19]

Hegel's understanding of the rabble, however, did not correspond exactly with the perspective of a conservative elite, as the existence of the mob was connected to that of the very rich.[20] The characteristics of each class were also linked; they shared a common "physical and ethical degeneration."[21] Thus, Hegel argued that "the rabble is distinct from poverty; usually it is poor, but there are also rich rabble."[22] These links and similarities were developed in the political thought of the middle classes and were used to challenge the place of the wealthiest members of society.

The ideological significance of the split between aristocratic and middle-class views of the mob is illustrated by the competition between the aristocracy and the revolutionaries to build social alliances with the poor majority of the population at the outset of the French Revolution.

Both sides attempted to exploit the illusion that a ferocious army of brigands, that is, a mob of beggars, vagabonds, and criminals, were roaming France in the Great Fear of 1789. The aristocracy blamed the brigands for the rioting and political unrest that had occurred, an explanation that was not simply a case of self-deception as it was calculated to turn the populace against those who would riot. By contrast, middle-class revolutionaries used the Great Fear to foment popular rebellion. They did so by encouraging a rumor that the brigands were in the pay of the aristocracy, an accusation that linked the mob with the wealthy elite.[23]

Both the conservative defenders of established elites and their middle-class opponents separated the mob from the people. But where conservatives also distinguished the elite from the people, while claiming that there was an identity of interests between them, the middle class identified themselves as the people, while linking the character and interests of the elite to those of the mob. The latter perspective conceived of social gradations as circular rather than linear. Thus, the very wealthy and the mob, who might appear to be at opposite ends of the social structure, were seen as similar. "The scum is perhaps as mean as the dregs," was how William Beckford put it.[24] In between were "the people . . . the middling people of England, the manufacturer, the yeoman, the merchant, the country gentleman, they who bear all the heat of the day . . . [and] have a right . . . to interfere in the condition and conduct of the nation."[25]

Beckford's distinction between the people and the low element of the mob, the dregs, was implicitly based on property ownership. In this respect, the mob appears to be conceived of as the *mobile vulgus*, as it is composed of the poor majority. What distinguishes the two concepts, however, is the social structure in which the mob is placed. The *mobile vulgus* was used to maintain a distinction between elite and mass; the people, however, belonged to neither group. Locating the people between these extremes meant that two opposing social categories became replaced by three graduated categories. At the same time, however, a dichotomous evaluation of these categories was retained. The virtuous people, with their legitimate claim to involvement in government, stood on one side; the mob, both rich and poor, stood on the other. This nominal distinction was not based on vertical social status, wealth, or property ownership, as in all these things the people were seen as standing between the rich and poor. Instead, the distinction was maintained by establishing connections between the two extremes that simultaneously separated them from the people.

One way in which this was done was to make the comparatively sympathetic argument that the actions of the elite had created a degraded class at the opposite end of the social spectrum, while the middle class had avoided this fate. This argument was adopted by Thomas Paine in his response to Burke's condemnation of the atrocities of the French Revolution:

> There is in all European countries a large class of people of that description, which in England is called the *Mob*. Of this class were those who committed the burnings and devastations in London in 1780, and of this class were those who carried the heads upon spikes in Paris. . . . It is by distortedly exalting some men, that others are distortedly debased, till the whole is out of nature. . . . In the commencement of a Revolution, those men are rather the followers of the *camp* than of the *standard* of Liberty, and have yet to be instructed how to reverence it.[26]

A second way in which the middle class could be separated from the classes that bordered it was on the grounds of a work ethic. The aims and attitudes of both rich and poor could be depicted as being opposed to the ordered, disciplined, systematic and prudent work habits and lifestyle of the middle classes.[27] The two explanations could be combined, as they were by Patrick Colquhoun. "The depraved habits and loose conduct of a great proportion of the lower classes of the people," Colquhoun explained, were partly due to their laziness and profligacy.[28] They were also, however, the fault of the rich, as "immorality, licentiousness and crimes are known to advance in proportion to the excessive accumulation of wealth."[29]

The social structure in which the middle class placed the mob can be pictured within a matrix where classes are divided on the basis of wealth and morality. These divisions are epitomized by the split between the propertied and propertyless classes on the one hand, and the hard-working and the lazy on the other. Both the middle class and the elite were propertied, but where the middle class worked hard, the elite were seen as being lazy. Insofar as the middle class also set itself in opposition to the mass of the population, this propertyless group was also depicted as lazy. The division between working hard and being lazy, however, made it possible for the middle class to identify with a much broader social base; those who were propertyless could also conceivably be hard-working and therefore could also be considered a part of the people.

Where the category of those who were hard-working and without property was identified as the core of the people, rather than as an adjunct to them, the ideological continuum shifted beyond middle-class opposition to vested elites to a more radical anti-capitalism. Such a transition is seen in the work of William Thompson. In a work published in 1824, Thompson contrasted "the peculiar vices of luxury and want" with the virtue of the middle class.[30] Three years later, however, this moral distinction became realigned to parallel the division between the propertied and propertyless; the split between "the Idle and the Industrious Classes" was seen as more or less synonymous with capitalist and worker.[31]

THE MOB AND MASS CONFLICT

It is now possible to return to the initial observation that explanations that attribute mass political action to the mob are false. Social historians, having established this falsity, have sometimes gone on to assume that the use of the mob in an ideological context is irrelevant to the objective attempt to explain mass conflict. George Rude, for example, concludes that "Taine's 'mob' should be seen as a frank symbol of prejudice, rather than a verifiable historical phenomenon."[32] It can be noted, however, that the ideology of historians who have used the mob to explain events is often not imposed on the events they study, but rather expresses the ideology of the period. Rude is right to point out that Taine's "vocabulary of expletives has served the conservative historians of the Revolution ever since."[33] Yet the extreme terms with which Taine characterized the revolutionaries were themselves derived from contemporary sources. This suggests the possibility that the import of Rude's conclusion should be reversed: The falsity of the mob as an explanation may emphasize its ideological importance to those who would influence mass action.

The assumption that the mob has had an ideological influence on political conflict allows the modification of one of the better established explanations of mass conflict in Britain and France in the late eighteenth and early nineteenth centuries: the argument that the pervasive accounts of mass action as coming from the mob conceal the development, from inchoate beginnings, of a coherent and autonomous working-class radicalism. The modification of this theory takes account of the ideological functions of the mob rather than dismissing the concept as mere prejudice, and this helps to explain some of the seemingly anomalous developments in the forms of mass conflict that have occurred in the late nineteenth century and beyond.

The theory that the mob is a statement of prejudice that conceals a growing workers' radicalism in the late eighteenth and early nineteenth centuries does not explain how the meaning of the mob shifted away from the *mobile vulgus* to become increasingly identified with an unproductive minority during this period. There is, to be sure, a suggestive similarity between the idea of inchoate mass action being replaced by fixed class objective on the one hand, and the explanation of this action as coming from the excitable, fickle, manipulated *mobile vulgus* being replaced by the purposively immoral mob on the other. But why should the idea of the *mobile vulgus* as the lowly majority of the population be replaced by the idea of the mob as a marginal unproductive minority? It would appear that, if anything, the reverse should be the case, as the *mobile vulgus*, a pejorative synonym for "the common people," identifies the object of prejudice with more descriptive accuracy than the mob.

There is a second problem raised by a theory that sees mob explanations as being rooted in prejudice against the emerging working class. Such a theory does not explain why the same concept appears in left-wing political doctrine, most notably in Marx's description of the lumpenproletariat.[34] This subject will be discussed in the next two chapters, which suggest that the lumpenproletariat mirrors conservative and middle-class depictions of socialists, not so much because Marx and Engels borrowed the concept from the bourgeoisie, but rather because they were competing against them in the attempt to direct mass action.

A final problem raised by the theory is that by concentrating on tracing the connections between earlier forms of inchoate mass action and their culmination in working-class radicalism, other connections, other branches of development, are ignored. After reading Rude and E. P. Thompson, two of the most convincing exponents of the theory, one is left with the impression that the subsequent history of mass political action must have been one that crystallized around left-wing objectives.[35] But as critics have pointed out, such action could also be counterrevolutionary, patriotic, jingoistic, and xenophobic.[36] Indeed, from the broader perspective of modern European history, to the extent that a cohesive working-class radicalism characterized the 1820s and 1830s, it appears not as the end of inchoate mass action so much as the lull before the storm.

Mass Subjectivity

The root of these problems lies in the assumption that the working class became increasingly autonomous. This assumption does not take sufficient account of the divergent ideologies that have influenced mass action in the nineteenth and twentieth centuries. The working class, along with other popular classes, has not been autonomous, but rather politically subjective.[37] The theory of increasing worker autonomy does not distinguish the object of working-class demands from the form in which these demands are expressed. By contract, if the masses are assumed to be politically subjective, their demands may indeed spring from the objective interests of a class without having a fixed form of expression. The aims of those engaged in mass action therefore are seen as having two components. They may be based on core interests or ideas, but this core can be channelled in any number of ways or mediated by other aims and beliefs.

The theory of increasing worker autonomy suggests that radical class demands became ever more established as the core of mass protest. It can be agreed that participants in mass action in the late eighteenth and early nineteenth centuries increasingly focused on demanding the political, social, and economic rights they believed they held as a result of their labor. But the development of a single main root of mass action should not be confused with uniformity in the direction such action might take.

The mob was one of the concepts that could be used to influence the direction of mass action rooted in the assertion of the rights of labor. The rights of labor were rights contingent on labor, which naturally leads to the establishment of a social and moral boundary between the productive and the unproductive. The distinction between social groups on the basis of their productivity certainly formed a pervasive element of working class and petit bourgeois propaganda against the rich.[38] The ideological potential of the mob lay in the fact that the same boundary could be extended to divide the poor.[39] Where conservatives used the word "mob" to describe participants in mass political action that threatened their interests, they were not therefore merely voicing their prejudices. If hostile mass action is publicly described as coming from the mob, and if the public believes it, it is possible to turn the public against this action.

It is now possible to identify the principle that explains and links the particular qualities that combine to create the ideological picture of the mob. The mob is made up of elements designed to conflict with the aims, values, self-image, and lifestyles of the poor majority in a society, while these elements still allow the mob to be identified from among the poor. Considered from this perspective, the mob becomes an immoral minority by definition, while its further qualities of being unproductive and parasitic place it in opposition to the interests of those who work and outside the rights of labor. The social characteristics ascribed to the mob and the alleged wickedness of its actions are thus calculated to conform to ideas of legitimacy and illegitimacy held by the poor majority. This is most clearly manifested in depictions of the mob as unproductive, although other features frequently associated with the mob, such as the claim that it has been bribed, serve to emphasize the illegitimacy of the actions with which it is associated.

If the mob can be used to generate widespread opposition to mass action, it can also be used to generate support, in the form of either (1) passive acceptance of measures taken against certain groups and their actions, or (2) active participation in these measures. Opposition and support are two sides of the same coin. The ideological rationale for propagating the picture of the mob is not, therefore, limited to being a reactive explanation of hostile mass action. The mob has been described as providing a false explanation of real events, but to use the mob for purposes of gaining popular support, it is not always necessary for an event to happen. The concept may also be used to identify the participants in a staged event, a persistent or looming threat, or a conspiracy. Because such depictions of the mob are divorced from any real threat, the groups that are attacked in such propaganda do not define themselves by their political stance and actions and may belong to any social category.

The mob performs a similar ideological function in defending beliefs as it does in promoting mass support. The difference is that the deception is internal rather than external. Any ideology in which the people are idealized, that is, seen as embodying the aims and values of the ideology, has difficulties in explaining mass political action opposed to these aims and values. Identifying such action with the mob is one way in which this idealized concept of the people can be kept intact; the belief is retained, even if the reality is different.

THE MOB AND THE PEOPLE

Once the ideological functions of the mob are identified, the shift from *mobile vulgus* to mob, the appearance of the mob in left-wing ideology, and the continuing diversity of mass action can be explained. The mob is not an anti-democratic term in the way that the concept of the *mobile vulgus* is anti-democratic. To describe hostile mass groups as the mob rather than as the *mobile vulgus* serves the aim, whether pragmatic or idealistic, of identifying an ideology with the interests of the majority.

It is true that the concept of the mob excludes unproductive groups from undertaking legitimate political action by identifying legitimacy with work. But by excluding such a minority, the rights of the working majority are recognized. The mob may appear to be a term of prejudice against the masses, either because its depiction of those engaged in mass conflict is spurious or because the distinction between the mob and the *mobile vulgus* is compounded by political commentators with an ambivalent attitude toward the bulk of the population. Nonetheless, to publicly identify the mob as an unproductive minority has an ideological appeal that can only be described as a democratic or populist one; it is an appeal to the people.

The switch from *mobile vulgus* to mob in descriptions of hostile mass action was indicative of developing doctrinal beliefs in the people, on the one hand, and a response to the increasing and potentially threatening power of mass groups on the other—a power that the French Revolution had graphically illustrated. From a middle-class perspective, the mob embodied qualities opposed to those of the people. From an elite perspective, the beauty of the mob as an ideological response to mass power was that it combined the repression of mass political action with the direction of mass political action. These two objectives could be combined with the mob precisely because it was a false explanation of the aims and composition of those who participated in mass protests.

The occurrence of the mob in left-wing political thought has been interpreted by some as a bourgeois aberration.[40] In fact, it can be seen to follow directly from the ideological functions of the concept. The boundary between the productive and the unproductive follows not only from demands for the rights of labor, but also from the belief in labor as "the foundation of human dignity."[41] This need not lead to the conclusion that the unproductive poor under capitalism are the mob; they may equally be viewed as victims of the system. The affinity between left-wing views on the virtues of productivity and the concept of the mob is revealed, however, when the question of what to make of the unproductive is projected into a utopian future. Michael Bakunin, for example, described how after the revolution, people would be free even to be lazy, but added:

> Society cannot, however, leave itself completely defenceless against vicious and parasitic individuals. Work must be the basis of all political rights. The units of society each within its own jurisdiction, can deprive such antisocial adults of political rights.[42]

The potential uses of the word "mob" to gain tacit or active mass support for conservative or middle-class doctrines is indicative of how the left, as well as the establishment, may be faced with hostile mass action. Therefore, use of the mob is not only consistent with left-wing beliefs but also enables the exponents of left-wing ideologies, like any other, to affirm their belief in the people in the face of mass opposition and to publicly characterize this opposition as coming from a wicked, unproductive minority.

Once the demand for the rights of labor is seen as having different forms of expression, the variety of ideological views that gained mass support in the late nineteenth century, including nationalist and racialist doctrines, becomes somewhat more comprehensible. The historical development of the demands for the rights of those who worked meant that religious and factional disputes did not continue unabated, but neither did they simply disappear. Such antagonisms could be recast in a way that recognized and expressed the idea of rights contingent on work. The ideological functions of the mob are significant to the tracing of such changes, because mob attributes could be applied virtually to any political, social, racial, or religious minority group within a society, including socialist agitators with their personal "dislike of all kinds of recognized labour . . . discipline and fatigue,"[43] decadent financiers engaged in an "orgy of luxurious debauch."[44] and parasitic Jews, "noxious members of the Body Politic, . . . [following] idle and useless pursuits."[45]

DEFINING THE MOB

This leads to the final point, which is that if the concept of the mob is defined in terms of its functions, what it is may be described differently, while what it does remains the same. The mob performs two functions in an ideology. First, it maintains the internal belief in the people. Second, it can be used to pursue the external objective of gaining or maintaining passive or active mass support. A functional definition of the mob is inseparable from the notion of the people, that is, the good, productive majority. This is not because the terms are defined through their relationship to each other, as bourgeoisie and proletariat might be. Neither is it because the mob is dependent on the people; it may be conceived of as socially parasitic, but it is politically independent. The connection lies in the importance of mass popularity to the realization of ideological objectives. The ideological concept of the mob from the late eighteenth to the late nineteenth centuries in Europe can thus be defined as the depiction of a wicked unproductive minority that is contrasted with the virtue and productivity of the majority as a means of establishing a harmony of interest with the majority. This definition emphasizes the conclusion that while the identification of those involved in political conflict as the mob is largely false, this does not demonstrate the concept's irrelevance to understanding mass action, but rather indicates its ideological importance in the attempt to influence such action. A case in point is provided in the next chapter.

NOTES

1. Alphonse de Lamartine, *History of the French Revolution of 1848*, trans. Francis A. Durivage and William S. Chase (Boston: Phillips, Sampson, 1851), vol.2, p. 188.

2. Pierre-Joseph-Victor de Besenval, Baron de Brunstatt, cited in Hippolyte Adolphe Taine, *The Origins of Contemporary France, The Ancient Regime*, trans. John Durand (New York: Henry Holt, 1896), p. 388.

3. J. Paul de Castro, *The Gordon Riots* (London: Oxford University Press, 1926), p. 31.

4. The Gordon riots, French Revolution, and other mass protests are discussed in George Rude, "The London 'Mob' of the Eighteenth Century," *Historical Journal* 2 (1959): 1–18; *The Crowd in the French Revolution* (Oxford: Clarendon Press, 1959); *The Crowd in History: A Study of Popular Disturbances in France and England 1730–1848* (New York: John Wiley, 1964). The events in France in 1848 are examined by Pierre Caspard, "Aspects de la lutte des classes en 1848: le recrutement de la Garde nationale mobile," *Revue Historique* 511 (July 1974): 81–106; Roger Price, *The French Second Republic: A Social History* (Ithaca, N.Y.: Cornell University Press, 1985); Mark Traugott, *Armies of the Poor: Determinants of Working-Class Participation in the Parisian Insurrection of June 1848* (Princeton: Princeton University Press, 1985).

5. Hippolyte Adolphe Taine, *The Origins of Contemporary France, The French Revolution*, 2 vols., trans. John Durand (New York: Henry Holt, 1896), vol. 2, pp. 125–26.

6. Karl Marx, "The Eighteenth Brumaire of Louis Bonaparte," in *Karl Marx Frederick Engels Collected Works*, 50 vols. (New York: International Publishers, 1975), vol. II, p. 149. This English translation of the collected works of Marx and Engels is henceforward referred to as *MECW*.

7. Nineteenth-century writers on degeneracy are discussed by Richard D. Walter, "What Became of the Degenerate?" *Journal of the History of Medicine and Allied Sciences* 11 (1956): 422–29.

8. Mob behavior was often seen as resulting from a combination of the participants' morality and the conditions under which they lived, although stress

was generally laid on the former explanation. H. A. Fregier, for example, concluded that the mob could be divided from the rest of the poor on the basis of its immorality. See *Des classes dangereuses de la population dans les grandes villes, et des moyens de les rendre meilleures*, 2 vols. (Paris: J. B. Bailliere, 1840), vol.2, p. 503.

9. Darwin cites the work of some of the first social Darwinists to investigate the mob in his discussion of the disturbing degree of fertility of "the reckless, degraded and often vicious members of society." See Charles Darwin, *The Descent of Man, and Selection in Relation to Sex* (London: John Murray, 1871), p. 174. The effect of social Darwinism on middle-class views of the mob in nineteenth-century England is discussed in Gareth Stedman Jones, *Outcast London* (Oxford: Clarendon Press, 1971), pp. 286–88.

10. Gustave Le Bon, *The Crowd: A Study of the Popular Mind* (London: T. Fisher Unwin, 1896).

11. William Watson, *A Decacordon of Ten Quodlibeticall Questions Concerning Religion and State*, 1602, reprinted as a facsimile in D. M. Rogers, ed., *English Recusant Literature 1558–1640*, vol. 197 (Ilkely, England: Scholar Press, 1974), p. 67. Other examples of the seventeenth- and eighteenth-century concept of the *mobile vulgus* are discussed in Christopher Hill. "The Many Headed Monster," in *Change and Continuity in Seventeenth Century England* (London: Wiedenfeld and Nicolson, 1974), pp. 181–220.

12. The etymological link between *mobile vulgus* and "mob" is discussed in Raymond Williams, *Keywords* (London: Fontana, 1976), p. 193. Another term related to "mob" was "the mobility," which was used to identify the unemployed among the poor in the late eighteenth and early nineteenth centuries. See Mark Harrison, "The Ordering of the Urban Environment: Time, Work and the Occurrence of Crowds 1790–1835," *Past and Present* 110 (1986): 134–68.

13. See Raymond Williams, *Culture and Society 1750–1950* (New York: Harper and Row, 1958), pp. xii, 298–99.

14. Edmund Burke, *Burke's Thoughts on The Cause of the Present Discontents* (London: Macmillan, 1902), p. 6.

15. William Cobbett, *Political Register* 25 July 1812, cited in Williams, *Culture*, p. 16. Emphasis in the original.

16. Edmund Burke, *Reflections on the Revolution in France*, ed. Conor Cruise O'Brien (Harmondsworth, England: Penguin, 1982), p. 173, fn66. O'Brien's footnote adds: "The indefinite article is important. Burke's opponents quoted him as referring to 'the swinish multitude.' . . . Burke, however, may have been referring to a particular type of multitude, with a particular occasion in mind." Burke, seizing on Dr. Price's description of voters in Britain as "the *dregs* of the people," levelled the same form of accusation against him: "You will smile here at the consistency of those democratists, who, when they are not on their guard, treat the humbler part of the community with the greatest contempt" (p. 146).

17. Castro, *Gordon Riots*, p. 39.

18. Georg W. F. Hegel, *Hegel's Philosophy of Right*, trans. T. M. Knox (London: Oxford University Press, 1967), addition 149 to paragraph 244.

19. Some of the ambiguous ways in which conservatives in the late eighteenth century depicted the mob both as the majority and as an idle minority are examined in Ellen Meiksens Wood, "The Myth of the Idle Mob," in *Peasant-Citizen and Slave: The Foundations of Athenian Democracy* (London: Verso, 1988), pp. 5–41.

20. Hegel, *Philosophy of Right*, paragraph 244.

21. Ibid., paragraph 185.

22. G.W.F. Hegel, *Vorlesungen über Rechtsphilosophie*, ed. K.-H. Iltung (Stuttgart: Frommann Verlag, 1974), vol. 4, p. 608. Translated and quoted in Allen W. Wood, *Hegel's Ethical Thought* (Cambridge: Cambridge University Press, 1990), p. 252.

23. Georges Lefebvre, *The Great Fear of 1789: Rural Panic in Revolutionary France*, trans. Joan White (London: New Left Books, 1973). Lefebvre also describes how the middle-class revolutionaries used brigands as an excuse to form militias to act against not only the aristocracy, but also the working class. Given the attendance of workers at revolutionary meetings, however, "it was not really possible to make this particular point clear" (p. 132).

24. William Beckford in the House of Commons, 13 November 1761. Cited in Lucy Sutherland, "The City of London in Eighteenth-Century Politics," in *Essays Presented to Sir Lewis Namier*, eds. Richard Pares and A. J. P. Taylor (London: Macmillan, 1956), p. 66. This speech is also mentioned in Rude, "The London 'Mob.' "

25. Sutherland, "City of London," p. 66.

26. Thomas Paine, *The Rights of Man* (London: J. M. Dent, 1915), pp. 32–33.

27. Max Weber, *The Protestant Ethic and the Spirit of Capitalism*, trans. Talcott Parsons (New York: Charles Scribner's Sons, 1958), pp. 163, 173–74, 179–80.

28. Patrick Colquhoun, *A Treatise on the Police of the Metropolis* (London: Joseph Mawman, 1800), preface, pp. 90, 311–12.

29. Colquhoun, *Treatise on Police*, Preface. An example of the malign influence of the rich was gambling, which, despite being "a horrid waste of useful time," was spread to the lower classes via servants who imitated the habits of their wealthy employers. See p. 150.

30. William Thompson, *An Inquiry into the Principles of Distribution of Wealth Most Conducive to Human Happiness: Applied to the Newly proposed System of Voluntary Equality of Wealth* (London: Longman, 1824), p. 259.

31. William Thompson, *Labor Rewarded*, "By One of the Idle Classes" (London: Hunt and Clarke, 1827), p. vi.

32. Rude, *The Crowd in the French Revolution*, p. 239.

33. Ibid., p. 2

34. The similarities between the lumpenproletariat and the mob are discussed by Frank Bovenkerk, "The Rehabilitation of the Rabble: How and Why Marx and Engels Wrongly Depicted the Lumpenproletariat as a Reactionary Force," *Netherlands Journal of Sociology* 20 (April 1984), pp. 13–41. Also see Traugott, *Armies of the Poor*, p. xiv.

35. George Rude, *The Crowd in the French Revolution*; "The London 'Mob,'" p. 18; *Ideology and Popular Protest* (New York: Pantheon Books, 1980); Edward P. Thompson, *The Making of the English Working Class* (New York: Random House, 1964); "The Moral Economy of the English Crowd in the Eighteenth Century," *Past and Present* 50 (1971): 76–136.

36. Robert J. Holton, "The Crowd in History: Some Problems in Theory and Method," *Social History* 3 (1978): 225. Also see Geoffrey Best's review, "The Making of the English Working Class," *The Historical Journal* 8 (1965): 271–81.

37. This concept is described in Helmut Dubiel, "The Specter of Populism," trans. Steven Stottenburg, *Berkeley Journal of Sociology* 31 (1986): 398–411.

38. An example is found in C. F. Volney, *The Ruins* (New York: Peter Eckler, 1890). In Chap. 15, a dialogue takes place between the people—"farmers, artifacers, merchants, all professions useful to society," and a privileged class that is found to be quite useless. Published as a tract, this chapter enjoyed wide circulation in the early 1800s. See Volney, *Ruins*, pp. 63–66; Thompson, *Working Class*, p. 99.

39. Illustrative of the popular recognition of such a division is an anonymous letter written during the Gordon riots:

> There is a mob on foot supported and encouraged by desining men to suport protestens and down with popery. But believe me Religin is not the cause for they are composed of house brakers pickpockets and all maner of wagerts. . . . If act was repaled the people wod soon setel the mob but present they dare not. (Castro, *Gordon Riots*, p. 178).

40. Bovenkerk, "The Rehabilitation of the Rabble," pp. 36–37.

41. Michael Bakunin, "Revolutionary Catechism," in *Bakunin on Anarchy*, trans., ed. Sam Dolgoff (London: George Allen and Unwin, 1973), p. 89.

42. Ibid., pp. 79–81. For other examples of the exclusion of the mob from a socialist utopia, see Edward Bellamy, *Equality* (New York: D. Appleton, 1897), pp. 362–64; Emile Pataud and Emile Pouget, *Syndicalism and the Co-operative Commonwealth* (*How we shall bring about the Revolution*) (Oxford: New International Publishing, 1913), pp. 151–52. Bakunin's sentiment sounds a little strange given that he also wrote:

> By the *flower of the proletariat*, I mean . . . that great *rabble of the people* (underdogs, "dregs of society") ordinarily designated by Marx and Engels in the picturesque and contemptuous phrase *Lumpenproletariat*, . . . the "riffraff,"

that "rabble" almost unpolluted by bourgeois civilization, which carries in its inner being and in its . . . collective life, all the seeds of the socialism of the future, and which alone is powerful enough to inaugurate and bring to triumph the Social Revolution. ("The International and Karl Marx," *Bakunin*, p. 294).

But once it is recognized that Bakunin is publicly accusing Marx and Engels of conceiving of the mob as the *mobile vulgus*, the anomaly is explained. The passage is one in which Bakunin reclaims the language identified as being used against the masses per se, while also purporting to show how they are perceived by his political rivals.

43. Joseph Conrad, *The Secret Agent* (London: Penguin, 1963), p. 82.

44. Karl Marx, "The Civil War in France" (First Draft, Second Draft and Address of the General Council), *Karl Marx Friedrich Engels Gesamtausgabe* (Berlin: Dietz Verlag, 1978), vol. 1, part 22, p. 104.

45. Colquhoun, *Treatise on Police*, p. 637.

CHAPTER 2

The Place of the Lumpenproletariat in Marx's Dialectic

The lumpenproletariat formed a vital element of Marx's theory as it was set down in *The Eighteenth Brumaire of Louis Bonaparte*. This analysis of Louis Napoleon's coup d'etat contained Marx's re-evaluation of his dialectical theory in the light of the violent revolutionary and reactionary events in Europe from 1848 to 1851. The problems that these events had presented to Marx's agenda, the realization of communism, were transcended by his derivation of a more comprehensive theory of social change through which the lumpenproletariat were placed in dialectical opposition to the proletariat.

There is a tendency to view the lumpenproletariat as being of little importance to Marx's theory.[1] By contrast, *The Eighteenth Brumaire* has often been seen as central to understanding Marx's conception of the state.[2] However, Marx's overriding concern in *The Eighteenth Brumaire* did not lie in analyzing the state as such but rather in affirming his theoretical belief in society's total transformation through an impending European revolution. Neither this belief nor the role of the lumpen-proletariat can be separated from other elements of Marx's analysis without distorting his process of reasoning.[3] To understand this process,

This chapter is a revised version of my article "*Utopia* and the Lumpenproletariat: Marx's Reasoning in *The Eighteenth Brumaire of Louis Bonaparte*," *Review of Politics* 50 (1988): 445–65.

it is necessary to see how and why Marx linked the lumpenproletariat with his expectation of revolution.

THE SOCIAL CHARACTERISTICS OF THE LUMPENPROLETARIAT

The lumpenproletariat was Marx's term for the mob. It referred to those who were propertyless, unemployed, and whose methods of securing a living placed them outside the productive process. In addition, Marx described members of the lumpenproletariat as having a distinct attitude, morality and mental state: They did not want to work, they were thieving, and given these propensities, they followed their immediate material interests without scruple. Given the axiom that the material circumstances of a class determined its state of consciousness, these aspects of the lumpenproletariat might have been regarded as complementary and self-contained. In fact, they formed a matrix.

In addition to those with both the material and mental attributes of the lumpenproletariat, Marx identified two further distinct groups composed of those who shared either its material position or its state of consciousness. Those who were without property and outside the relations of production might nonetheless share the consciousness of the class to which they formerly belonged. This group was the surplus population. Conversely, those who did not share the material position of the lumpenproletariat, in that they owned capital, might nonetheless share its mental state. This group contained the finance aristocracy.

The contrast between the attitudes of the surplus population and the lumpenproletariat involved the logical recognition that material circumstances were neither the invariable nor immediate determinants of consciousness, and that, furthermore, this was the case not only at the level of individuals but also of entire social groups. To explain how people with similar material circumstances had different states of consciousness, Marx used the concepts of corruption and degeneration over time. The lumpenproletariat and surplus population were seen as having been forced out of their former occupations and thence out of the relations of production. Although people under such circumstances might initially retain their class consciousness, their new material position made them susceptible to agents of corruption. Furthermore, the longer that they stayed outside the productive process, the more likely it was that they or their descendants would degenerate, lose their former class consciousness, and adopt instead the lazy, thieving attitudes congenial to their conditions of life, relating to society only through their interests in taking products from it without engaging in productive relations.

In *The Communist Manifesto*, Marx and Engels wrote:

> The "dangerous class," the social scum, that passively rotting mass thrown off by the lowest layers of old society may, here and there, be swept into the movement by a proletarian revolution; its conditions of life, however, prepare it far more for the part of a bribed tool of reactionary intrigue.[4]

This description placed the lumpenproletariat outside the dialectical process described in the *Manifesto*: the struggle between classes to retain or revolutionize the modes of production through which they were defined. The lumpenproletariat's conditions of life were not intrinsically affected by the processes centered around production, with the result that they were, in themselves, neither revolutionary nor reactionary.[5] Thus, Marx argued that the lumpenproletariat had no common interest in the form of society and did not constitute a class defined in this sense. Its members were a class only insofar as they were lumped together by their last point of contact with the dialectic, their common exclusion from the relations of production. As the mode of life of the lumpenproletariat lay outside productive relations and the resulting class relations, it was not at stake in a revolution. Therefore, the lumpenproletariat would join the side in a revolution that offered them the greatest material inducement.

Marx found confirmation of this analysis of the lumpenproletariat in the revolutions of 1848. He wrote: "In Paris [in June] the mobile guard, in Vienna 'Croats'—in both cases *lazzaroni*, lumpenproletariat hired and armed—were used against the working and thinking proletarians."[6]

Working and thinking, a place in the relations of production, and the class consciousness it engendered encapsulated the distinction between proletariat and lumpenproletariat. Meanwhile, the original Neapolitan *lazzaroni* demonstrated a lumpenproletarian lack of distinct class interest by fighting not with the bourgeoisie but against them on behalf of the monarchy.[7]

Where the lumpenproletariat sided with the proletariat, as they had in the February 1848 revolution in Paris, at least some of them did so out of their immediate individual interests. These were the professional conspirators described by Marx in an 1850 article for the *Neue Rheinische Zeitung*.[8] Marx wrote that the conspirators' activities were not motivated by any class interest in revolution, but rather by an interest in stealing or begging a living from the proletarians they recruited, while revolution was engaged in for the thrill of the thing. These conspirators attempted to force an artificial revolution where material conditions were not ripe. This lack of recognition of the material causes of revolution was not just a mistake; it was a consequence of the conspirators' withdrawal from participation in the dialectic through their withdrawal from work. Thereby, any proletarian consciousness that they might have had had degenerated or been corrupted by the police. Marx described the tavern-frequenting conspirators as "either workers who have given up their work and have as a consequence become dissolute, or characters who have emerged from the lumpenproletariat [bringing] all the dissolute habits of that class with them into their new way of life."[9]

Truly proletarian revolutionaries did not share the immediate interests of the professional conspirators; by advancing the interests of their class rather than themselves, they looked to the future realization of these interests through the transformation of society.

In *The Class Struggles in France*, Marx identified a further lumpenproletarian element that had supported the February revolution. These were the youths subsequently recruited into the mobile guard by the bourgeois provisional government. They gave their allegiance to the bourgeoisie in the proletarian revolt of June 1848 because the bourgeoisie paid them to, and after the insurrection was defeated, "the *Mobile Guards*, found their reward in the soft arms of the courtesans."[10] Marx contrasted the mobile guard with workers who had lost their jobs as a result of the crisis. These workers could not be bought by the provisional government through their state employment in work gangs. Their consciousness was still a proletarian one even while their unemployment made their societal position analogous to that of the lumpenproletariat at the point of their recruitment.[11]

The Finance Aristocracy

In June 1848, the proletariat had been provoked into revolution by the bourgeoisie in order that the working class might be crushed. In February 1848, however, the bourgeoisie had allied with the proletariat and all other classes to depose the finance aristocracy. Marx's explanation of the February revolution revealed the flexibility of the concept of the lumpenproletariat and its utility in fitting events to theory. Just as the distinction between proletariat and lumpenproletariat had been used to explain splits among the urban poor in 1848, so a similar distinction could be made between the wealthy of society. In *The Class Struggles*, Marx used this distinction to explain that the violent change of government in February was not a proletarian revolution, although it advanced the conditions necessary for this revolution to take place. Although the implications of the analysis would be altered in *The Eighteenth Brumaire*, the way in which the lumpenproletariat was fitted into the interpretation of events remained the same. In itself unaffected by the dialectical relationship between the forces and relations of production, the lumpenproletariat could still be invoked as an agent of change in the political sphere.

Given schematically, Marx's argument was as follows: Only under the industrial bourgeoisie do the means and relations of production of advanced capitalism develop. Therefore, a successful proletarian revolution can only occur against a form of state rule that incorporates the industrial bourgeoisie.[12] The February revolution was not a successful proletarian revolution. For it to have been so, it would have had to have been against the industrial bourgeoisie. In fact, the revolution was against the finance aristocracy, which was not part of the industrial bourgeoisie. Therefore, it necessarily failed to turn into a successful proletarian revolution. However, by allowing the consolidation of a general bourgeois rule, the February revolution put into place the ruling element against which the proletarian revolution would occur and thereby advanced the dialectic.

Marx viewed the finance aristocracy as quite unlike the industrial bourgeoisie. Living by gambling, they did not provide an impetus to the materialist dialectic. They became "rich not by production but by pocketing the already available wealth of others," opposed to the interests of the productive bourgeois and adopting a style of life "where money, filth and blood comingle. The finance aristocracy, in its mode of acquisition as well as in its pleasures, is nothing but the *rebirth of the lumpenproletariat at the heights of bourgeois society*."[13] The industrial bourgeoisie deposed the finance aristocracy in February, only to readmit them into a shared power that combined bourgeois interests against those of all other classes. In doing so, they defined the forces of oppression against which the revolution would take place, a revolution that would be supported by all oppressed classes against the entire bourgeoisie.

DIALECTICAL AND UTOPIAN THEORY

Marx compared his idea that communism would be obtained through a dialectical process of proletarian revolution in opposition to their class oppressors with "*utopia, doctrinaire Socialism*," described as "an *application of systems*, which the thinkers of society . . . devise." By contrast, a true revolution would lead to:

> the *abolition of class distinctions generally*, to the abolition of all the relations of production on which they rest, to the abolition of all the social relations that correspond to these relations of production, to the revolutionising of all the ideas that result from these social relations.[14]

This was a description of a revolution against the dialectically created conditions of bourgeois society. However, it was not a revolution in dialectical opposition to the lumpenproletariat. As has been seen, the lumpenproletariat played no part in the relations of production and were not defined as a class in this sense. Their social relations were unrelated to the relations of production and so their ideas were not the result of their position within productive society. In short, the lumpenproletariat, by living outside society, outside the relations of production, and outside the dialectic before the revolution, might remain as a blot upon communist society after the revolution. *The Eighteenth Brumaire* contains within it Marx's implicit recognition of this deduction. His response was to reverse his earlier description of the last stage of capitalist society.

More's Utopian Solution to Indigence and Idleness

Despite Marx's rejection of utopian thinkers, the thought processes behind his analysis of Louis Napoleon's coup can be compared with those of Thomas More in his writing of *Utopia*. This comparison helps to explain why Marx linked the lumpenproletariat to the proletarian revolution. It compares the use of the idea of a perfect society to structure not only *Utopia* but also *The Eighteenth Brumaire*, and the obstacle the concept of the lumpenproletariat or mob presented to the realization of such a society in each work. More described a state of affairs that would preclude the existence not only of the destitution condemned at *Utopia's* outset, but also of beggars, vagabonds, and criminals, that is, the lumpenproletariat. This same purpose underlay Marx's analysis of Louis Napoleon's coup d'etat. In this sense, *The Eighteenth Brumaire* was Marx's *Utopia*.

The distinctions Marx used to place the lumpenproletariat within a social matrix were similar to those used by More. On the one hand, there was the split between those who owned property and those who did not; on the other, between those who desired to work and those who were lazy. Beggars, vagabonds, and criminals were assigned to either of the propertyless categories. More distinguished those who wanted work but were unable to find it from those who were inclined to be idle. Utopia was designed to deal with the economic conditions and the deficiencies of character that gave rise to both types of people. The common distribution of life's necessities in Utopia meant that no one need beg.[15] Work was not only available to but also compulsory for all.[16] Although few laws were said to be required in Utopia, they included punitive measures against unauthorized travel, that is, vagabondage.[17] The laws were also designed to deal with criminals of evil character, in a system where money and property, the basis for much of the crime outside Utopia, had been abolished.[18]

More, like Marx, identified gambling, prostitution, and tavern drinking as lumpenproletarian activities, for those who were drawn to participate in such activities by inclination were impoverished by them and so induced into a life of theft.[19] These activities were made absent from Utopia.[20] The rich, who elsewhere conspired to rule in their own interests against those of the poor, were also excluded from Utopia.[21] In particular, More singled out the idle wealthy, distinguished by their lack of participation in productive activity. Among members of this class, More described "a ryche goldesmythe, or an usurer, or to bee shorte anye of them, which either doo nothing at all, or els that whyche they doo is such, that it is not very necessary to the common wealth."[22]

More identified some beggars, vagabonds, and criminals as peasants who had been turned off the land in order that it could be used for sheep farming.[23] Two additional sources of such people were soldiers and nobles' retainers. The mode of life of these latter groups predisposed them toward lazy, thieving inclinations while preparing them for no productive activity. As a result, those who were dismissed from or invalided out of service were forced by necessity to practice the only profession for which they were fitted—a life of theft. Theft was interchangeable with soldiering, "so wel thees. ii. craftes agree together."[24]

More contrasted the threat that these armed groups posed to European societies with Utopia, which was without a standing army. However, More also explained that the Utopian system was not universal to the region in which it was placed. Thus, when it was necessary to conduct a war, the Utopians would bribe mercenary soldiers to support them. Although these mercenaries would sell themselves to the highest bidder, their character also made them enthusiastic combatants. Those who survived to receive their pay squandered it in debauchery. The Utopians' opinion of them was that "they should doo a verye good deade for all mankind, if they could ridde out of ye worlde all that fowle stinking denne of that most wicked and cursed people."[25]

Marx's Dialectical Solution To The Lumpenproletariat

More had designated a lumpenproletarian group in essentially the same terms as Marx's. Both of them saw the lumpenproletariat as an undesirable segment of society and wished to be rid of it. But communist society after the revolution, the utopia foreseen by Marx, could not, for theoretical reasons, be described as More had done. Marx could not sketch out laws that would punish a lumpenproletarian lifestyle under communism.[26] Yet, as Marx and More concurred, given that there were some who were idle and corrupt through choice, it was not enough for material conditions to change in a way that ensured a lumpenproletarian way of life was no longer necessary for the survival of those who followed it. They might continue to follow it anyway. This was the problem that Marx's analysis of events from 1848 to 1850 had left him. In the coup d'etat of Louis Napoleon, he saw its solution.

The coup, Marx decided, signified the bourgeoisie's irrevocable handing of state power to the lumpenproletariat. The lumpenproletariat were thus readmitted en masse into the dialectic. The final proletarian revolution against capitalist society would be one against lumpenproletarian rule rather than that of the bourgeoisie. Therefore, the revolution and subsequent dictatorship of the proletariat would be one opposed not only to bourgeois relations of production, but also to all that characterized the lumpenproletariat. By reincorporating the lumpenproletariat into a dialectical process whereby communism was to be obtained through opposition, Marx had removed criminals, beggars and vagabonds from his utopia.

MARX'S ANALYSIS OF LOUIS NAPOLEON'S COUP

In analyzing the coup d'etat, Marx repeated his earlier descriptions of the class struggles in France since 1848, even though the conclusions that he drew were different. He described again how the united class revolution against the finance aristocracy in February 1848 had been followed by a united counterrevolution against the proletariat in June. This had been effective in breaking the strength of the proletariat's revolutionary opposition, rendering it inactive in the subsequent class struggles. The bourgeoisie had then proceeded to attack its erstwhile supporters in June, by acting against the political power of the petit bourgeoisie and oppressing the peasantry. The united bourgeoisie, represented by the "Party of Order," had thus established its most absolute power over French society.[27]

Marx contrasted this period of bourgeois parliamentary rule (with its motto, "Property, family, religion, order"[28]) with the executive rule of Louis Napoleon after the coup. This rule was also one of absolute power, but it was power held by the lumpenproletariat,[29] under a leader who threw "the entire bourgeois economy into confusion."[30] With the lumpenproletariat in power, Marx described how bourgeois representatives:

> are . . . thrown into dungeons or sent into exile; their temple is razed to the ground, their mouths are sealed, their pens broken, their law torn to pieces. . . . Bourgeois fanatics for order are shot down on their balconies by mobs of drunken soldiers, their domestic sanctuaries profaned, their houses bombarded for amusement—in the name of property, of the family, or religion and of order.[31]

This attack, with its accompanying systematic political repression was "the final and complete collapse of the rule of the bourgeoisie."[32] The transformation from its rule to that of the lumpenproletariat was a transformation from rule designed for bourgeois exploitation of all other classes to rule designed primarily for theft from all classes without exception. Although the social structure of France was still based on bourgeois relations of production, for the lumpenproletariat had become the only class without interests in systemic opposition to them, it was not bourgeois rule but the rule of the lumpenproletariat against which the proletarian revolution would occur.

Marx gave two seemingly contradictory explanations as to why the bourgeoisie had lost power to the lumpenproletariat. The first was that it had been the inevitable result of a dialectical process[33]; the second was that it was the result of mistakes on the part of the bourgeoisie. This apparent inconsistency was due to Marx's consistent underlying purpose of explaining the coup d'etat as the progression of the state apparatus into its final stage before the revolution.

Marx argued that the extraparliamentary bourgeoisie had been mistaken in believing that the executive rule of Louis Napoleon would leave their private interests undisturbed and provide them with tranquility.[34] They had also had an exaggerated perception of the threat posed by the economic recession through which they were passing. This was widely believed to be the prelude to a socialist revolution, one that would occur upon the expiration of Louis Napoleon's presidential term of office. Against this prospect, anything was preferable. Thus, Marx contrasted "the judgment of the English bourgeois with the prejudice of the French bourgeois." Where the former examined the economic bases of the recession, the latter, in the face of political events, "madly snorts at his parliamentary republic: *'Rather an end with terror than terror without end!'* "[35]

However, at the same time, Marx explained that events in France were the inevitable result of bourgeois support for the bureaucracy, and the measures the bourgeoisie took to undermine parliamentarism. The latter actions were in the political interests of the bourgeoisie insofar as parliamentary government, by definition, involved opposition, and opposition would ultimately be expressed in revolution.[36] Similarly, Marx explained that the scale and pervasiveness of the bureaucracy were in the material interests of the bourgeoisie, as within the bureaucracy "it finds posts for its surplus population and makes up in state salaries for what it cannot pocket in the form of profit, interest, rent, and honorariums." Thus, the bourgeoisie supported the "extensive state machine in its numerous ramifications" (implicitly including the army), at the same time as the conditions for parliamentarism were being abolished.[37] This resulted in a situation in which the bureaucratic and military elements of the state could depose parliament without arousing opposition, as the forces of parliamentary opposition had already been broken.[38]

This raises two questions. First, what relationship did Marx see between the mistakes of the bourgeoisie and the inevitability of developments leading to Louis Napoleon's coup? In other words, was the fact that most of the bourgeoisie between 1848 and 1851 came to support Louis Napoleon, and hold a distorted view of their economic position and the immediacy of the socialist threat, incidental to the political and material determinants of the coup, a result of these determinants, or in itself an essential aspect of the change in power?

Second, was the bureaucratic and military rule after the coup seen by Marx to have been, of necessity, a lumpenproletarian one, or was this a quirk of history not integral to the sequence of events?

In answer to the first question, the apparent blunders of the bourgeoisie were mistakes only insofar as they were premature; that is, their economic fears, fears of revolution, and support of the executive were ultimately well grounded. Thus, Marx did not hold that the coup had been inevitable in the sense of being an inevitable occurrence within a particular time period. It was, however, inevitable in that it formed part of an inevitable sequence of events. Had the French bourgeoisie been more judgmental, events in France would not have occurred at the time they did but would have occurred nonetheless.

To answer the second question, it is necessary to begin by stepping back from its focus on the lumpenproletariat. It has been argued that Marx was using his analysis of Louis Napoleon's coup to reincorporate the lumpenproletariat into the dialectic. However, this was only part of his general theoretical reincorporation of the population outside the productive process into the process of history. This in turn was linked to the radicalization of the peasantry. Not only the lumpenproletariat but also the peasantry stood between the proletariat and the full realization of a communist utopia. It was the peasants who had voted for Louis Napoleon in 1848, and it was they who endorsed him in the plebiscite held after the coup. To solve this problem, Marx formed a common connection between the lumpenproletariat, the peasantry, and a third group, the surplus population. This group became the pivotal reference point of his analysis.

In *The German Ideology*, Marx and Engels wrote that vagabonds and other lumpenproletarian types were not special products of bourgeois society but members of a group that had "existed in every age and who existence *on a mass scale* after the decline of the Middle Ages preceded the mass formation of the ordinary proletariat."[39] Members of this group had been forced into their way of life by the breakdown of the social and economic bases of feudal society. Like More, Marx and Engels identified their origins among discharged soldiers and retainers as well as peasants who had been forced off their land so that it could be turned into pasture. However, once these people had been excluded from a place in the structure of mainstream society, many chose to retain their new lifestyle. The alternative was to be absorbed by the nascent manufacturing industries, where vagabonds "were only prevailed upon to work with the greatest difficulty and through the most extreme necessity, and then only after long resistance."[40]

Thus, Marx had identified the transition from feudalism to capitalism as one in which part of the population was forced off the land or sacked, and then, through legislation or for survival, forced into manufacturing. Such people in transition were not unambiguously lumpenproletarian. They formed a surplus population, composed of those who shared the marginalized economic status of the lumpenproletariat as well as those who subsequently held lumpenproletarian attitudes.

In England, Marx saw the transition process between the rural and urban population as a continuing one. There, the proletariat, as described in the *Manifesto*, was steadily becoming "the immense majority." However, in France a different process was taking place. The root of the difference lay in the way capitalism had emerged in each country. Whereas in England the bourgeoisie had gained power through the expropriation of peasant lands, in France the bourgeoisie consolidated their power over the nobility by the granting of property rights to the peasantry.[41] The contradictions Marx identified in the peasants' position in capitalist society had progressively impoverished them.[42] However, the state of French industry, weaker than that of England and unable to compete with it during the depression of 1851,[43] did not allow the peasants' absorption into the urban proletariat. Thus, the fate of peasants forced from their small holdings was not proletarianization, but marginalization in the growing surplus population. As Marx described it:

> To the four million (including children, etc.) officially recognised paupers, vagabonds, criminals and prostitutes in France must be added five million who hover on the margin of existence and either have their haunts in the countryside itself or, with their rags and their children, continually desert the countryside for the towns and the towns for the countryside.[44]

The peasantry fed into the surplus population, and the threat of their marginalization became the threat Marx predicted would radicalize them. The army and the bureaucracy were drawn from the surplus population "[reaching] out for state offices as a sort of respectable alms."[45] Thus, the bureaucracy and the army were drawn from a group outside the relations of production and were susceptible to being lumpenproletarian. This was not an inherent feature of either group; Marx explained that both had been engaged in productive relations under Napoleon I.[46] It was, however, inherent to the dialectic Marx had formulated in *The Eighteenth Brumaire*, that in order for the peasantry to become radicalized, they first had to lose their faith in executive government. This executive government was, by necessity, non-productive and divorced from holding class interests other than those of the lumpenproletariat, for the same conditions that created the marginalized surplus population that would finally radicalize the peasantry were the conditions that provided recruits for the bureaucracy and army.[47] This recruitment process was supported by the bourgeoisie who, unable to absorb the ruined peasants into manufacturing, also had a "surplus" of their own class living off state posts. Therefore, the parasitic lumpenproletarian state apparatus was not an incidental feature of the state under Louis Napoleon but was inseparable from the radicalization of the peasantry.

The Eighteenth Brumaire was the presentation of an alternative route to communism in countries whose peasantry, while becoming marginalized, were not then becoming urbanized. The development of the capitalist system in France, insofar as it was defined as development toward an ultimate revolution, had progressed to the penultimate stage. This stage went beyond the pure rule established by the bourgeoisie after 1848, as Louis Napoleon's lumpenproletarian regime, by alienating the peasants from executive rule, would give *"the proletarian revolution . . . that chorus without which its solo becomes a swan song in all peasant countries."*[48] However, it was the distinct nature of French events that Marx predicted would have consequences extending far beyond France's borders. All of continental Europe had been brought to capitalism as a result of the revolution of 1789. All Europe had "tremble[d] at the June earthquake" of 1848.[49] Similarly, the proletarian revolution destined to occur in France would provoke a revolution throughout Europe. Therefore, although Marx did not see French events as providing a model of universal historical development—as was argued by Lenin[50]—he did see them as an agent of such development.[51]

LAMARTINE

It has been seen that with considerable intellectual dexterity, Marx was able to combine the existence of the lumpenproletariat and surplus population, and the predominance of the peasantry in France, with the apparently reactionary turn of events after June 1848 to create a dialectical theory that reaffirmed his belief in an inevitable proletarian revolution. Before concluding this chapter, however, it can be noted that *The Eighteenth Brumaire* was not written, as it is now read, simply as a historical and academic analysis, but also as a persuasive and rhetorical pamphlet. Despite Marx's emphasis on the inevitability of a revolutionary conflagration, he still believed that *The Eighteenth Brumaire* helped to fan the flames. In this case however, the rhetorical features of the work implicitly contradicted the analysis it contained.

In analyzing revolutionary events in *The Eighteenth Brumaire*, as in other works, as inevitable, Marx ostensibly stressed that revolutionary crowds always had a particular class composition: They were formed either by a single class or by a class alliance. Furthermore, these classes had fixed interests, even if, as in the case of the lumpenproletariat, this interest was merely theft. Class alliances could be maintained only so long as class interests coincided. At a theoretical level, therefore, Marx denied the idea that revolutionary crowds might be treated as irreducibly socially heterogeneous with interests that were subjective and flexible. At the same time, however, the popular appeal of the concept of the lumpenproletariat was one that reached out to exactly this type of heterogeneous, subjective group. An example can be inferred by returning to the writings of the orator Lamartine,[52] whose populist rhetoric endeared him neither to Marx nor to the French aristocracy.[53] Marx described how Lamartine, "the spokesman of the February Revolution, according to both his position and his views belonged to the *bourgeoisie*."[54]

Lamartine, historian, poet, and minister in the 1848 provisional government, described his own views as favoring class unity. Writing in exile after the coup, he related in heroic detail his encounters with the Parisian crowds of 1848 and his recruitment of the youthful mobile guard. This timely act, said Lamartine, preempted the possibility that the new recruits would be led astray by sinister political opponents.[55] For although the crowds in Paris included honest working men—mistaken in their socialist beliefs but with hearts that were gentle and true—circulating among them was a party of vicious communists, whose supporters Lamartine described as follows:

This party had for its army, besides its enrolled and fanatical disciples, . . . all that ignorant, floating and unsettled portion of the vagrant population. . . . Everything which stagnates becomes corrupt. . . . [C]onspirators . . . in the secret societies could recruit their forces only from the deep mephitic mud of the population of great capitals. Crime only ferments in these agglomerations of idleness, debauchery, voluntary misery and vice; the immorality removed from open day, where the discipline and labor of society does not penetrate. . . . [F]reed convicts, abject in their manners, stagnating in vice, . . . men vomited from jails, . . . those, in fine, who are themselves the personification of the constant whirl of dissipation, of the unceasing breath of agitation, of the luxury of chaos and the thirst of blood.[56]

The epithets, the metaphors, the filth are all rendered in terms identical to Marx's description of the lumpenproletariat, but are used to describe the opposite side.

This raises the question whether Marx's or Lamartine's analysis was right. The answer, it might be suspected, is: Neither. Lamartine's rhetoric was too bound up with his idealization of the people to admit that some of them might oppose him. Marx's attribution of political action to the lumpenproletariat is viewed with skepticism because his concept of this class parallels the questionable idea of the mob. It can also be noted that studies of the social composition of the mobile guard—whose enlistment records have survived—have found it to have been predominantly working class.[57] In this respect, it can be suggested that Marx's identification of the lumpenproletariat provided a helpful method of denying that mass subjectivity played a part in the events of 1848–51 in favor of an analysis based entirely on class interest and class struggle.

This conclusion renders the implications of the similarities between Marx's and Lamartine's rhetoric more acute. Lamartine's language is excited and emotive. It is language that might appeal to a socially heterogeneous crowd without fixed interests by providing a generic picture of a hated group outside all classes and beyond the bounds of a moral and productive society. It can be asked, therefore, whether Marx's analysis might, ironically, have been designed to have a similar appeal at a rhetorical level, and whether Marx used the lumpenproletariat not only to deny mass subjectivity, but also to take advantage of it. We will return to these questions at the end of the next chapter, which takes a closer look at the social structure underlying Marx's analysis of events in France.

NOTES

1. See for example, Tom Bottomore, "Lumpenproletariat," in *A Dictionary of Marxist Thought*, ed. Tom Bottomore (Oxford: Basil Blackwell, 1983).

2. Theories of Bonapartism, class equilibrium, and state autonomy have all been drawn from *The Eighteenth Brumaire*. See Hal Draper, *Karl Marx's Theory of Revolution*, 2 vols. (New York: Monthly Review Press, 1977); Frederick Engels, *The Housing Question* (New York: International Publishers, 1935); Vladimir Lenin, "The State and Revolution," in *V. I. Lenin Collected Works* (Moscow: Progress Publishers, 1964), vol. 25, pp. 381–492; Nicos Poulantzas,

Political Power and Social Classes, trans. Timothy O'Hagan et al. (London: New Left Books, 1973); Leon Trotsky, *The Struggle Against Fascism in Germany* (New York: Pathfinder Press, 1971).

3. For the argument that, on the contrary, Marx's expectation of revolution can be separated from his analysis of events in France, see Engels's 1895 "Introduction" to Marx, *The Class Struggles in France 1848–1850* (New York: International Publishers, 1964), pp. 10–13.

4. Karl Marx and Frederick Engels, "The Manifesto of the Communist Party," *MECW*, vol. 6, p. 494.

5. Hal Draper, who devoted an interesting and thorough chapter to the lumpenproletariat, traced Marx's idea that, in economic terms, the lumpenproletariat were excluded from societal dynamics to the *Paris Manuscripts*. See Draper, *Marx's Theory*, vol.2, pp. 453–78.

6. *MECW*, vol. 7, p. 505.

7. Ibid., vol.8, p. 17.

8. Ibid., vol.10, pp. 311–25.

9. Ibid., p. 317.

10. Ibid., p. 76.

11. Ibid., pp. 62–63.

12. Ibid., p. 56.

13. Ibid., p. 51. Emphasis in the original.

14. Ibid., pp. 126–27. Emphasis in the original.

15. *Utopia*, trans. Ralph Robinson, ed. Edward Arbor (London: Edward Arbor, 1869), pp. 97, 157–58. Marx quoted from this edition of *Utopia* in *Capital*.

16. *Utopia*, p. 86.

17. Ibid., p. 96.

18. Ibid., pp. 121–22, 127–28, 160. More's attitude toward property and crime is expanded in "In Lutherum," in *Utopia*, trans. Paul Turner (Harmondsworth: Penguin Books, 1961), p. 149.

19. *Utopia*, p. 43.

20. Ibid., pp. 97, 112.

21. Ibid., pp. 159–60.

22. Ibid., p. 158.

23. Ibid., pp. 40–42.

24. Ibid., p. 39.

25. Ibid., p. 137.

26. Marx mentions the incompatibility between such prescriptions and "scientific socialism" in *The Eighteenth Brumaire*. See *MECW*, vol. 11, p. 142.

27. Ibid., pp. 109–110, 129, 131–133, 137, 140, 146, 181–82, 187–89.

28. Ibid., p. 111.

29. Ibid., p. 182.

30. Ibid., p. 197.

31. Ibid., p. 112.

32. Ibid., pp. 182, 183 Note c. This plainly contradicts Poulantzas's interpretation of the lumpenproletariat as a supporting class of a bourgeois power bloc under Bonapartism (*Political Power*, p. 243).

33. *MECW*, vol. 11, p. 177.

34. Ibid., pp. 143, 184.

35. Ibid., pp. 175–76.

36. Ibid., pp. 139, 141–43.

37. Ibid., p. 139.

38. Ibid., p. 137.

39. *MECW*, vol. 5, p. 202.

40. Ibid., p. 69.

41. Marx's distinction between society in Britain and France is well explained in Poulantzas, *Political Power*, pp. 174–75.

42. *MECW*, vol. 10, pp. 120–21; vol. 11, pp. 189–93.

43. *MECW*, vol. 11, pp. 163, 173–75.

44. Ibid., p. 191.

45. Ibid.

46. Ibid., pp. 190–91, 191 Note b.

47. For another interpretation, see Poulantzas's argument that the bureaucracy Marx described in *The Eighteenth Brumaire* held a "juricio-political bourgeois ideology" that could be traced back to More and Niccolo Machiavelli, and that "bureaucratism," and not "simple material interests," conditioned the state apparatus's support for Louis Napoleon (*Political Power*, pp. 216–18, 358–59).

48. *MECW*, vol. 11, p. 193 Note b. This implies that in *The Eighteenth Brumaire*, Marx viewed the question of the perpetuation of the capitalist economic system in France only in terms of the time it would take before the peasants became radicalized. This can be contrasted with the argument that Marx was explaining how a capitalist system perpetuated itself under an apparently independent state apparatus by distinguishing between social and political power.

49. *MECW*, vol. 11 p. 111.

50. Lenin, *The State and Revolution*, pp. 409–10. Lenin cited Engels's "Introduction" to the third edition of *The Eighteenth Brumaire* in support of this view.

51. Marx's idea that a European revolution would begin in France has been traced to his early writings on Hegel by J. L. Talmon, *Political Messianism* (New York: Frederick Praeger, 1960), pp. 213–14.

52. More, Marx, and Lamartine are discussed in Karl Mannheim, *Ideology and Utopia*, trans. Louis Wirth and Edward Shils (New York: Harcourt, Brace and World, 1936), pp. 200–203. Marx and Lamartine are discussed extensively by Talmon.

53. Addressing Lamartine, and accusing him of having "lied knowingly" about the crowd, Count Horace de Viel Castel wrote: "The people are robbers, and every successful revolt, since glorified in your writings, was achieved by persons who looked to disorder for means of larceny." See *Memoirs of Count Horace de Viel Castel*, trans. Charles Bousfield (London: Remington, 1888), vol. 1, p. 15.

54. *MECW* vol.10, p. 53.

55. Alphonse de Lamartine, *History of the French Revolution of 1848*, trans. Francis A. Durivage and William S. Chase (Boston: Phillips, Samson, 1851), vol. 1, pp. 170–172.

56. Pierre Caspard, "Aspects de la lutte des classes en 1848: le recrutement de la garde nationale mobile," *Revue Historique* 511 (July 1974), pp. 81–106.

57. These studies include Caspard; Roger Price, *The French Second Republic: A Social History* (Ithaca, N.Y.: Cornell University Press, 1985), pp. 166, 185, 187; Charles Tilly and Lynn H. Lees, "The People of June 1848," in *Revolution and Reaction*, ed. Roger Price (New York: Harper and Row, 1975), pp. 170–209; Mark Traugott, *Armies of the Poor: Determinants of Working-Class Participation in the Parisian Insurrection of June 1848* (Princeton: Princeton University Press, 1985).

CHAPTER 3

Marx's Class Analysis of Events in France

In the last chapter, we focused on the way Marx explained Louis Napoleon's coup of 1851 by incorporating the lumpenproletariat into the dialectic. Although this chapter covers some of the same ground, its aim is not to provide a comprehensive account of a specific analysis, but rather to discern Marx's method of explanation and its relationship to his ideological objectives. To do this, it is necessary to examine all three of his major works on France—*The Class Struggles in France, 1848–1850; The Eighteenth Brumaire of Louis Bonaparte*; and *The Civil War in France*—to identify how the lumpenproletariat formed part of an underlying class structure that Marx left implicit in his writings. It might be thought that this class structure would be found in Marx's abstract works. In fact, if a class structure is taken directly from Marx's writings on France, it can be seen to differ from the class analysis Marx presented in abstract works not only in its form and its assumptions, but also in providing the basis for a potentially effective cross-class ideological appeal.

A RECONSTRUCTION OF MARX'S CLASS STRUCTURE

In the *Communist Manifesto*, Marx presented a polarized view of classes under capitalism. The bourgeoisie and proletariat were described as being diametrically opposed to one another, while other classes were subsumed within this clash of opposites. Engels summarized this polarization in a footnote to the *Manifesto*: The bourgeoisie owned the means of production, while the proletariat did not; the bourgeoisie were employers, while the proletariat were their employees.[1] However, this simple polarization was, in itself, insufficient to explain the events that surrounded the deposition of Louis Philippe of France in the February Revolution of 1848. First, the bourgeoisie had engaged in internal struggles; second, the proletarian insurgents of June 1848 had been opposed by the mobile guard, a newly formed militia recruited from among the Paris poor.

Marx's explanation of these events in *The Class Struggles* redefined the relationship between the proletariat and the bourgeoisie in a way that would provide a framework for class analysis in *The Eighteenth Brumaire* and *The Civil War*. Instead of being viewed in polarized terms, the two classes were defined in terms of intersecting class attributes.

Marx's structural shift from polarized to intersecting class attributes entailed two consequences. The first was that the proletarian and bourgeois classes were not necessarily antithetical, but could differ from each other in one respect while being similar in others. The second consequence was that an intersecting structure allowed Marx to analyze events in terms other than an overriding split between bourgeoisie and proletariat.

Marx's first step in the process of shifting from a polarized to an intersecting class structure was to explain bourgeois support for the February Revolution by distinguishing between different groups within the bourgeois class:

> It was not the French bourgeoisie that ruled under Louis Philippe, but *one faction* of it: bankers, stock-exchange kings, railway kings, owners of coal and iron mines and forests, a part of the landed proprietors associated with them—the so-called *finance aristocracy*.[2]

Marx separated the finance aristocracy from the rest of the bourgeoisie by explaining that they became wealthy not by being engaged in productive activity but rather by financial speculation: manipulating stock and bond prices "to . . . the ruin of a mass of small capitalists and the fabulously rapid enrichment of the big gamblers."[3]

Marx continued to explain why the mobile guard had attacked the proletariat in June 1848. As has been seen in Chapter 2, he did so by defining the members of the mobile guard as lumpenproletarian. Despite being propertyless, members of this class shared some characteristics with the finance aristocracy: Both gained their living outside the productive process and both displayed "unhealthy and dissolute appetites."[4]

It is now possible to see how Marx had outlined a class structure that defined the place of the finance aristocracy and lumpenproletariat as well as the bourgeoisie and proletariat. The finance aristocracy and lumpenproletariat were similar in that neither was involved in the productive process. These two groups were distinguished from the bourgeoisie and proletariat because both of these latter classes were engaged in production. This structural distinction, between the finance aristocracy and lumpenproletariat on the one hand and the bourgeoisie and proletariat on the other, did not in itself require that a distinction be drawn between employer and employee, as both criteria indicated involvement in production.

From a second perspective, the lumpenproletariat and proletariat were similar in that neither owned property; this distinguished them from the bourgeoisie and finance aristocracy, who were both property owners. Here again, however, the polarized class analysis of the *Manifesto* had been revised. The finance aristocracy could be described as a "faction" of the bourgeoisie not because it owned productive property but because it had the potential to do so; it was the fact that the finance aristocracy directed its wealth toward gambling rather than production that made it a separate faction of the property-owning class.

The finance aristocracy differed from the bourgeoisie in a further respect: Its "unhealthy and dissolute appetites" indicated that it was degenerate. The degeneracy of the lumpenproletariat separated it from the proletariat in a similar manner. Marx's analytic understanding of degeneracy was that a degenerate was not interested in making a living through being involved in the productive process, but rather aimed to make a living outside this process. More loosely, Marx associated degeneracy with vice, which he defined in fairly conventional moral terms. By contrast, a non-degenerate had an interest in being involved in production and, although obscured by the capitalist system, this interest was not merely an instrumental one, but included the aim of participating in production for its own sake.

The structural separation of the non-degenerate bourgeoisie and proletariat from the degenerate finance aristocracy and lumpenproletariat was, like the previous distinctions, one that indicated a structural similarity within each pair. Although the bourgeoisie and proletariat held different

Figure 1
Marx's Class Categories I

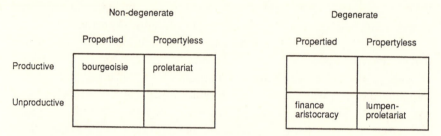

interests, at a level of analysis that distinguished degenerate from non-degenerate aims, these interests were alike insofar as they could both be realized through some form of participation in production. The interests of the lumpenproletariat and finance aristocracy were also alike in being disassociated from production.

The structure that Marx used to define the place of the bourgeoisie, proletariat, finance aristocracy, and lumpenproletariat is summarized in Figure 1. This diagram presents three class attributes: property, productivity, and aims. These attributes have each been bifurcated, using nominal distinctions, to yield six class characteristics. The property attribute is bifurcated into being wealthy enough to own productive property or being too poor to own productive property. The productivity attribute is bifurcated into being involved in production or not being so involved. The aims attribute is bifurcated into having an interest in the act of production or having no interest in the act of production. In Figure 1—and in all subsequent diagrams—these characteristics are labelled propertied or propertyless, productive or unproductive, and non-degenerate or degenerate.

The eight boxes in Figure 1 indicate that the combination of the three bifurcated class attributes yields eight possible class categories. A class category is defined as a social group that has three class characteristics, each belonging to a different attribute, in any combination. Class categories are different from particular classes in two ways. First, they are different because more than one class may be contained within a single class category. For example, not only members of the bourgeoisie but also of the petit bourgeoisie and peasantry fall into the category of those who have property, are productive, and have a producing interest. The second difference between class categories and specific classes is that more than one category may be used to define a single class. Marx's description of the finance aristocracy as a faction of the bourgeoisie provides an example of this.

At this stage in our reconstruction of the class structure found in *The Class Struggles*, the distinctions between being productive and non-degenerate and between being unproductive and degenerate appear to be unnecessary. To distinguish among the bourgeoisie, proletariat, finance aristocracy, and lumpenproletariat, it is sufficient to combine the property attribute in a matrix with either one of the productivity or aims attributes. To explain why the distinction between productivity and aims is made in Figure 1, it is necessary to consider two further categories, one containing the surplus population, the other containing the big bourgeoisie. The first of these categories was critical to the analysis in *The Eighteenth Brumaire*, while the second was critical to *The Civil War*.

The surplus population had no property and did not produce, yet had an interest in being involved in production. In other words, their lack of productivity was involuntary, and they belonged in the category of propertyless, unproductive non-degenerates. By extension of the same reasoning, it can be understood why the combination of being propertied, unproductive, and non-degenerate did not form a category in Marx's class analysis. If a social group with sufficient wealth to own productive property did not engage in the productive process, they could not be said to be productive involuntarily. Therefore, their aims did not include an interest in being involved in production, and they were necessarily degenerate.

To say that an unproductive property owner is necessarily degenerate is not to say that a productive property owner is necessarily non-degenerate. Although we have described the finance aristocracy as falling within a single class category of unproductive, propertied degenerates, Marx's descriptive list of the members of the finance aristocracy, cited above, included members of a second category of productive, propertied degenerates. Members of this category can be labeled "big bourgeoisie," a term that Marx used interchangeably with "finance aristocracy" in *The Class Struggles*. In *The Civil War*, this category of productive, propertied degenerates acquired a distinct significance. In this work, the bourgeoisie of the Second Empire was described as engaged in production merely for the sake of lavish consumption and other degenerate reasons:

Bourgeois society . . . attained a development unexpected even by itself. Its industry and commerce expanded to colossal dimensions; financial

Figure 2
Marx's Class Categories II

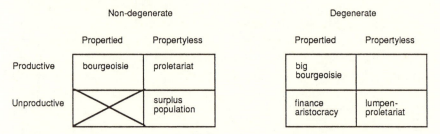

swindling celebrated cosmopolitan orgies; the misery of the masses was set off by a shameless display of gorgeous, meretricious, and debased luxury.[5]

It is now possible to modify Figure 1 in two stages. The first stage, shown in Figure 2, presents a more developed summary of Marx's class categories. This diagram adds the categories containing the big bourgeoisie and surplus population. It also crosses out the contradictory combination of propertied, unproductive non-degenerates. The second stage is to present Marx's categories in a diagram that indicates the relationship among these categories. This is shown in Figure 3.

In the matrix shown in Figures 1 and 2, the bifurcation of class attributes is indicated by intersecting vertical and horizontal lines that separate the two opposing class characteristics that compose each attribute. Figure 3 uses lines in the same way; the only difference is that they lie at an angle to each other. For example, the categories containing the proletariat, bourgeoisie, and big bourgeoisie all lie above the line that separates being productive from being unproductive. Therefore, these three categories are productive. The finance aristocracy, lumpenproletariat, and surplus population categories all lie below the same line and are therefore defined as unproductive.

It has sometimes been remarked that Marx's works on France, in particular *The Eighteenth Brumaire*, represent a departure from the simple class antagonisms described in the *Manifesto*.[6] The class structure that has been reconstructed here shows how this was done. Marx replaced his description of a class structure based on the polarization of the bourgeoisie and proletariat with classes defined through three intersecting class attributes. Apparently, polarized classes still had a place in the class structure insofar as class categories that were opposite each other shared

Figure 3
Marx's Class Structure

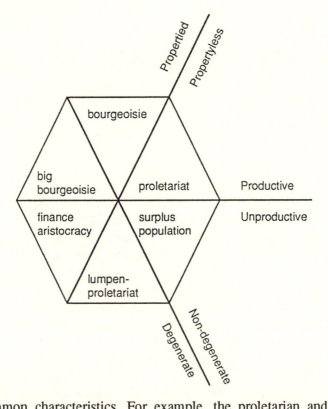

no common characteristics. For example, the proletarian and finance aristocracy categories had completely different class characteristics. This form of polarity, however, was no long embodied in the structural relationship between the bourgeoisie and the proletariat, as their class categories were adjacent to each other. Adjacent categories shared two out of three class characteristics, while categories one step removed from each other shared one characteristic out of three. Thus, the bourgeois and proletarian categories both contained productive non-degenerates and differed only with respect to property ownership. On the other hand, the bourgeois and surplus population categories, one step removed from each other, shared only an interest in the act of production.

The structure shown in Figure 3 not only shows class category distinctions but also illustrates a relationship that Marx sometimes saw among all six categories. This relationship was one in which the level of wealth Marx associated with each category decreased in a clockwise direction from the finance aristocracy to the lumpenproletariat. But why should the combination of nominal divisions yield an ordinal scale of wealth? To answer this question, each class attribute is considered in turn.

The property attribute concerned wealth directly. By definition, the three propertied categories were wealthier than the propertyless proletariat, surplus population, and lumpenproletariat. A second class attribute, productivity, had different effects on the wealth levels of the propertied and propertyless categories. The only propertyless category whose members were also productive, the proletarian category, was wealthier than the other two propertyless categories. By contrast, among the propertied categories, the unproductive category of the finance aristocracy was wealthier than the other two propertyless categories containing the big bourgeoisie and bourgeoisie. The comparative wealth of the proletarian category can be explained by recalling that the lack of involvement in production by members of the surplus population was involuntary. One of the reasons this was so was economic; the surplus population aspired to enter into the productive process because this would improve their standard of living. The lumpenproletariat were also poorer than the proletariat, as although they did not aim to work, they otherwise stood in the same structural relationship to the proletariat as did the surplus population. The relationship between wealth and productivity was reversed among the propertied classes; although members of each propertied category had sufficient wealth to be able to engage in production, they did not all have sufficient wealth to be able not to engage in production. As has been seen in Marx's description of the successful speculation of the finance aristocracy at the expense of smaller capitalists, in order to be unproductive while retaining propertied status, it was necessary to have sufficient funds to manipulate the financial markets.

It remains to be explained why degenerate productive property owners were wealthier than their non-degenerate counterparts, and why, among those who were unproductive and had no property, the degenerate lumpenproletarian category was the most impoverished of all. Marx's justification for these distinctions lay in the association he drew between the level of wealth possessed by a social category and its aims.

In *The Protestant Ethic and the Spirit of Capitalism*, Max Weber described the Puritan view that extreme wealth was corrupting, as it encouraged the wealthy to see no virtue in work. At the other end of the scale, those who begged were also seen as corrupt, as they too were unwilling to work. Marx drew a connection between degeneracy and extremes of wealth and poverty for broadly similar reasons. The extreme poverty of the lumpenproletariat signified its degeneracy, its voluntary lack of participation in production. Where Marx distinguished among different strata within the surplus population, the lumpenproletariat were compared with its lowest layer, the paupers.[7] Similarly, among the productive propertied classes, those whose aims included an interest in production had not been corrupted by a high degree of wealth; hence, the comparative wealth of the degenerate big bourgeoisie.

THE FLEXIBILITY OF THE STRUCTURE

Frank Bovenkerk criticized Marx's concept of the lumpenproletariat by listing five different definitions of it found in his work. These were first that it was "a historical remnant of an earlier society"; second, "a group of individual social degenerates"; third, "part of the general proletariat"; fourth, "a category outside the economic system"; and fifth, "an odd mixture of miscellaneous other definitions."[8] With the exception of the first—which refers to the description of the lumpenproletariat in the *Manifesto*—these definitions correspond fairly well with the characteristics associated with the lumpenproletariat in the intersecting class structure. Thus, the second definition corresponds to its degeneracy, the third to its lack of property, the fourth to its lack of productivity, and the fifth to combinations of these characteristics. Bovenkerk's criticism of these different meanings of the lumpenproletariat as confused and contradictory has some validity on purely theoretical grounds. Nonetheless, Marx's various characterizations of the lumpenproletariat were not the result of a careless analysis but were designed to link it to a broader class structure. The advantage of this intersecting class structure was that it provided a framework that allowed Marx considerable flexibility in his interpretation of French events. The reconstruction of Marx's class structure makes it possible to explain this flexible method of analysis in formal, abstract terms. This formal description of a flexible class analysis can then terms. This formal description of a flexible class analysis can then provide the basis for Marx's application of this method in his explanation of events.

Marx's flexible class analysis has as its premise two implicit propositions not always associated with his thought. The first proposition is that it is possible to use multiple definitions of a class to explain events. The second proposition is that it is possible that groups of people may act differently even though they have the same material circumstances within the same society.[9] In the intersecting class structure, such differences require distinguishing the actions of those who are degenerate from those who are not.

Once the possibilities of multiple class definitions and of different actions by groups having similar circumstances are accepted, the intersecting class structure can be made flexible if combinations of the three class attributes are used sequentially rather than simultaneously. To examine the extent of this formal flexibility, it can be noted first that no single class characteristic is sufficient to define the other two characteristics that compose a class category. For example, members of the bourgeoisie, big bourgeoisie, and finance aristocracy categories are all wealthy enough to own property, but are otherwise divided between whether or not they are productive and whether or not they are degenerate. However, since the eight class categories shown in Figure 1 have been reduced to six categories in Figure 3, each class category has two characteristics that define it. These are the characteristics whose dividing lines separate a category from its two adjacent categories. An example, discussed earlier, is the surplus population category, whose members are defined by being unproductive and non-degenerate and whose lack of property follows as a consequence of these two class characteristics. But although only two class characteristics are required to define any one category, each of the six class characteristics is a necessary component in defining two of the three categories that embody its dimensions, each time in combination with a characteristic belonging to a different class attribute. In short, all three class attributes are necessary in order to distinguish between the six class categories.

At this point, the technique Marx used to analyze events through the intersecting class structure can be introduced. This technique consists of shifting between different combinations of class attributes in order to group class categories in various ways as well as to step between them.

The structure allows for seven basic combinations of attributes with which to explain class divisions from different perspectives. The first combination is one that uses all three class attributes simultaneously in an analysis of society. This is shown in Figure 3. However, six more combinations are possible if one or two attributes are ignored. These combinations are shown in Figure 4. Three of these combinations in fact use only one attribute and thus group three categories. Three more combine two attributes. These combinations group adjacent pairs of the categories that are not defined by the characteristics of the two attributes

Figure 4
Perspectives on Class

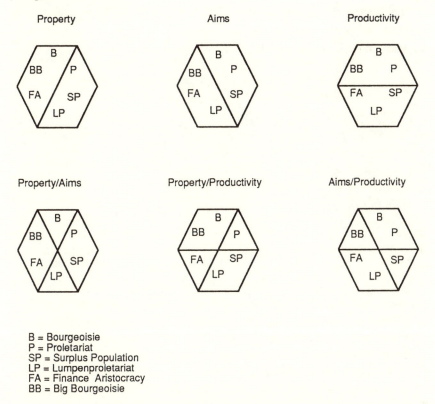

B = Bourgeoisie
P = Proletariat
SP = Surplus Population
LP = Lumpenproletariat
FA = Finance Aristocracy
BB = Big Bourgeoisie

Class attribute divisions correspond with the ones shown in Figure 3.

that are being combined. Therefore, in an explanation of events, two or three categories may be grouped by disregarding one or two distinguishing class attributes. Furthermore, to explain events in terms of a series of class formations, motivations, and alliances, it is possible to shift from one combination of attributes to another. For example, class categories that have been grouped together may subsequently be distinguished from each other by shifting to a combination of attributes that reaffirms the divisions between them.

This technique of explaining events can also be described in terms of stepping between class categories. A step can be made that links any categories that are not opposite to one another by using one or two common characteristics. In the course of an explanation of events, it is possible to take a sequence of such steps.

EXPLANATION OF EVENTS IN FRANCE

The flexibility allowed by the intersecting class structure was critical to Marx's explanation of events in all three of his main works on France. To show how he used this flexibility, each work is examined in turn.

The Class Struggles

In *The Class Struggles*, Marx described the rulers of France before the February Revolution as belonging to the categories of propertied degenerates. This enabled him to explain why members of the bourgeoisie had combined with other classes in the February Revolution: From the perspective of the aims attribute, they were grouped with these classes through their common opposition to their rulers' degeneracy. Thus Marx described how:

> the non-ruling factions of the French bourgeoisie cried: *Corruption*! The people cried: *A bas les grands voleurs*! *A bas les assassins*! when in 1847, on the most prominent stages of bourgeois society, the same scenes were publicly enacted that regularly lead the *lumpenproletariat* to brothels, to workhouses and lunatic asylums, to the bar of justice, to the dungeon and to the scaffold. The industrial bourgeoisie saw its interests endangered, the petty bourgeoisie was filled with moral indignation, the imagination of the people was offended.[10]

Yet in explaining events after the February Revolution, Marx shifted his perspective from the degenerate or non-degenerate aims of classes to whether or not they possessed property. From this perspective, Marx explained that the Republic established after the revolution allowed, "beside the finance aristocracy, *all the propertied classes* to enter the orbit of political power."[11]

The distinction between propertied and propertyless classes separated the bourgeoisie from the proletariat, allowing Marx to return to an analysis based on a polarized understanding of class antagonisms. Part of the overall flexibility of Marx's class analysis was due to the fact that intersecting class divisions did not exclude the possibility of using a polarized class structure. He could switch between intersecting and polarized understandings of property divisions, making it possible to shift from one analytic approach to another. Second, the intersecting structure contained categories wholly opposite to each other; this allowed a certain continuity to be established when shifting between a polarized and an intersecting class structure.

The Eighteenth Brumaire

In *The Class Struggles*, Marx predicted that France's bourgeois government would fall to its polar opposite in a proletarian revolution. In the event, it fell to Louis Napoleon. To explain the 1851 coup, Marx again used an intersecting class structure rather than a polarized one. Within this structure, Louis Napoleon was identified as belonging in the category opposite to the bourgeois category: He was a member of the lumpenproletariat.[12]

Marx's identification of Louis Napoleon as the head of a lumpenproletarian state apparatus that had overthrown the representatives of the bourgeoisie raised the question of why the bourgeoisie had allowed this apparatus to grow. Marx's answer to this question has been considered in detail in Chapter 2. Here, however, it can be added that his argument involved two steps within the intersecting class structure. The first step was to link the bourgeoisie with the state apparatus by referring to the interests the bourgeoisie shared with members of the category containing the surplus population. Thus, Marx explained that the bourgeoisie supported the state apparatus prior to the coup, as "here it finds posts for its surplus population and makes up in the form of state salaries for what it cannot pocket in the form of profit, interest, rent and honorariums."[13] This was Marx's only explicit reference to the surplus population of the bourgeoisie in *The Eighteenth Brumaire*. But from *The Civil War*, one infers that he was referring to family members of the bourgeoisie.[14] Members of the surplus population category, insofar as their aims were not degenerate, could, almost by definition, be said to hold the same aims as the class from which they had been made surplus. In other words, although the surplus population was in a separate class category, it did not hold separate class aims. Marx relied on this link between the bourgeoisie and its surplus population to argue that the state apparatus was in bourgeois interests.

The next step that Marx took was to explain not why the state apparatus shared bourgeois aims, but why it opposed these aims. To do this, Marx shifted his perspective to examine the characteristics that grouped members of the surplus population category with the lumpenproletariat. Thus, the surplus population was described as being composed of ruined peasants, poor and propertyless, for whom state positions were a source of "alms"; that is, these positions were unproductive.[15] On the basis of these similarities, Marx shifted his characterization of the aims of the state apparatus to the degenerate thieving interests of the lumpenproletariat. Thus, in the conclusion to *The Eighteenth Brumaire*, Marx described how, after the coup, the bourgeoisie were robbed, imprisoned, and shot at, under conditions of disorder and anarchy.[16]

The Civil War

In *The Civil War* Marx explained that the bourgeoisie expanded and benefited under the Second Empire, indicating that he had revised his opinion of Louis Napoleon's rule in the 20 years since the coup. Marx's revision took the form of shifting the locus of class rule from the lumpenproletarian category to the finance aristocracy category.

Marx did not distinguish the Second Empire from the Third Republic that replaced it. The Republican government at Versailles, far from being different from the second Empire, was its summation. This was the government that the Paris Commune opposed. Where the locus of the Versailles government was the finance aristocracy, the Commune's locus was in the opposite category of the proletariat. Both of these opposing categories, however, allied with adjacent categories: The Versailles government was composed of the three degenerate categories, while the Communards included non-degenerate, productive property owners. Thus, Marx split the two opposing groups in Versailles and Paris along the line that separated degeneracy from non-degeneracy. This division is evident in the contrast Marx drew between those who left Paris under the Commune with those who remained:

> The party of disorder, whose regime toppled under the corruption of the Second Empire, has left Paris, . . . followed by its appurtenances, its retainers, its menials, its state parasites, its mouchards, its "cocottes", and the whole band of low *boheme* (the common criminals) that form the complement of that *boheme of quality*. But the true vital elements of the middle classes, delivered by the workmen's revolution from their sham representants, has . . . separated from it and come out in its true colours, . . . disavowing Versailles and marching under the banners of the Commune.[17]

Therefore, while degenerates, with or without property, supported the Versailles government, the Commune was supported by the "middle classes." Marx used this term to mean not only members of the petit bourgeoisie, but also capitalists of the "middling bourgeoisie."[18] Those capitalists in Paris who opposed the Commune were qualified as being wealthy capitalists.[19]

Given Marx's theory that history advanced through class conflict over the productive process, a degenerate outlook, by being disassociated from production, could in a sense be said to exhibit a lack of class consciousness. However, this should not be taken to imply that by degeneracy Marx meant that consciousness had not yet been reached. To be degenerate meant rather to have gone beyond any consciousness that included an intrinsic interest in production. Hence, the lumpenproletariat were a corruption of the surplus population, and, in a similar manner, Marx described the degenerate bourgeoisie of 1871 as a corruption of the middle class in the period of the French Revolution.[20] Thus, the degeneracy with which Marx characterized the bourgeoisie was not a fixed quality; it was a progressive one that he associated with increasing levels of wealth. In fact, Marx's use of the term "middle class" in *The Civil War* was synonymous with the category of non-degenerate, productive property owners. Marx used the term "bourgeoisie" to refer either to productive, propertied degenerates or to members of this category combined with the adjacent category of unproductive, propertied degenerates. Marx had shifted his definition of the bourgeois class, while the categories that undergirded this shift remained the same.

Throughout *The Civil War*, Marx frequently referred to the "state parasites" of the Second Empire and Versailles government. From a polarized class perspective, it might be thought that the entire bourgeois class was parasitic, because it appropriated what the proletariat produced. By using an intersecting class structure, however, Marx identified parasitism only with unproductive, degenerate categories. In other words, parasitism did not mean exploitative but productive relations between the bourgeoisie and proletariat, but rather referred to a lack of involvement in production. Although the bourgeoisie were despotic, they were not parasitic.[21] Nonetheless, by shifting between different combinations of class attributes, Marx was able to explain middle-class support for the Commune in terms of middle-class opposition to unproductive parasitism, while also explaining that this same opposition on the part of the Commune was an attack on bourgeois property relations.

To explain these shifts, it is helpful to remember that the term "middle class" refers to members of the non-degenerate category, which, following Marx's earlier usage, we have labeled "bourgeoisie" in the diagrams. And the term "bourgeoisie" refers to the degenerate categories we have labeled "big bourgeoisie" and "finance aristocracy." Bearing these meanings in mind, Marx first explained middle-class support for the Commune by combining the productivity and aims attributes. From this perspective, Marx argued that the middle class supported the Commune because its members were opposed to the lack of involvement in production and the degeneracy of the state apparatus represented at Versailles. Marx then shifted to consider the split between the Commune and Versailles solely in terms of the aims attribute. From this perspective, Marx was able to group the productive bourgeoisie with the parasitic class categories through their common characteristic of degeneracy. Having made this link, Marx was then able to argue that by revolutionizing the state apparatus, and "by doing away with the unproductive and mischievous work of the state parasites," the Commune was beginning the task of liberating the proletariat from exploitative bourgeois property relations.[22] In short, Marx explained middle-class support for the Commune by excluding the property attribute from his perspective, and then argued that the Commune attacked bourgeois property by linking possession of property to unproductive degeneracy.

MARX'S REASONING

The reasoning that Marx used in his writings on France can be analyzed in two steps. The first step is to consider his method of explanation in isolation; the second is to consider it in the context of underlying beliefs. Marx's method of explaining events in France is marked by flexibility, by the ability to shift between different perspectives of what defines a class and what accounts for class groupings. Considered in the abstract, it follows that the greater the flexibility allowed by the class structure, the greater the possibility of being able to explain events within the structure. However, underlying Marx's development of the structure, was not the aim of explanation per se, but rather of explanation within the context of two particular core beliefs. These beliefs limited the flexibility of the structure by establishing the boundaries that an explanation of events could have while remaining compatible with them. Marx's flexible method of explaining events was not, therefore, fully adaptive, as core beliefs added an essentialist element to it. Although the assumption that classes were polarized may have been too inflexible to explain events in France, there was also the possibility that the intersecting structure, if not limited, would become too flexible.

The limits of flexibility in the intersecting structure were due, in part, to the bifurcated attributes that were specific to it: productivity and aims. Marx's belief in communism as a state of free productivity that would be realized through class struggle accounts for his use of these particular attributes in developing the intersecting structure upon the property division of his polarized analysis. By dividing classes in capitalist society in this way, Marx was able to analyze events in terms of opposition between class categories whose characteristics, in a general sense, either affirmed or denied the form of a future communist society in which people would engage in production (affirmed or denied by the productivity attribute), and would do so freely (affirmed or denied by the aims attribute).

Second, Marx believed that the proletariat was the revolutionary agent of communism. One consequence of this belief was that it prompted the development of the structure in the first place in order to separate the working class from other mass political actors. After 1848, Marx's belief in the revolutionary working class made it imperative to be able to make such a separation. Throughout Europe, revolutionaries who could be interpreted as advancing the cause of communism faced mass opposition that extended beyond the ranks of the bourgeoisie. The intersecting class structure allowed Marx to separate this reactionary opposition from the working class, both because of the analytic distinctions that were made between those who were propertyless, and because of the shifting perspectives through which events could be interpreted.

Marx's belief in the revolutionary agency of the proletariat also served to limit the number of categories in the structure. There is one empty category in Figure 2, the category of productive, propertyless degenerates. In Figure 5, this seventh category is incorporated into Marx's intersecting class framework and labeled "degenerate workers." However, Marx did not add this seventh category to his intersecting structure, even though to have done so would have increased the formal flexibility of his method of explaining events by providing seven rather than six categories, four of which could not be defined by two characteristics but only by three. To admit the seventh category would be to call into question the belief in the revolutionary mission of the proletariat, which had prompted the development of the structure in the first place.

This is not to say that such a category necessarily conflicts with Marxist beliefs. Following Converse, Sartori, and Weber,[23] there does not have to be a necessary logical relationship between beliefs and the structure of an ideology, and in fact, Marxists have used such a category in explanations

Figure 5
Degenerate Workers

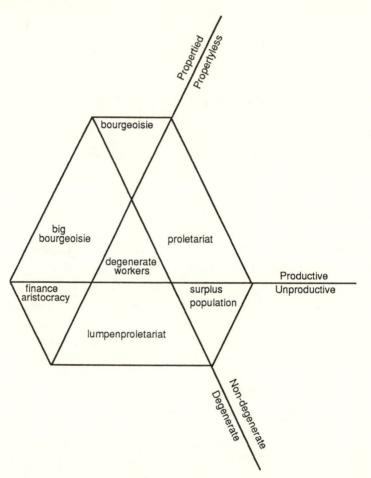

of the Soviet Union.[24] The argument is rather that Marx's development
of the intersecting structure was not directed at replacing his polarized
analysis with a more sophisticated and complex analysis per se, but
was instead directed toward undertaking the minimum divergence from
a polarized analysis that was necessary in order to affirm his core beliefs
in face of developments in Europe, and in particular, in France. The polarized
analysis of the *Manifesto*, although insufficient to explain events in France
after 1848, had, at a theoretical level, affirmed these core beliefs in
certain and straightforward terms. Marx's problem after 1848 was to
explain events in France by using a class analysis of increased complexity

without introducing an ambiguity that might detract from the certainty of his beliefs. The intersecting class structure provided the solution.

THE APPEAL TO THE PEOPLE

In his description of the class composition and ideology of demonstrators against the bourgeois French government on 13 June 1849, in *The Eighteenth Brumaire*, Marx wrote:

> As against the coalitioned bourgeoisie, a coalition between petty bourgeois and workers had been formed, the so-called *Social-Democratic* party. . . . The peculiar character of Social-Democracy is epitomised by the fact that democratic-republican institutions are demanded as a means, not of superseding two extremes. capital and wage labour, but of weakening their antagonism and transforming it into harmony. . . . [T]he democrat, because he represents the petty bourgeoisie, that is, a *transition class*, in which the interests of two classes are simultaneously mutually blunted, imagines himself elevated above class antagonisms generally. The democrats concede that a privileged class confronts them, but they, along with all the rest of the nation, form the *people*. What they represent is the *people's rights*; what interests them is the *people's interests*. Accordingly, when a struggle is impending, they do not need to weigh their own resources too critically. They merely have to give the signal and the *people*, with all its inexhaustible resources, will fall upon the *oppressors*.[25]

These latter comments about "the indivisible people,"[26] are, of course, ironic. Classes acted as a single unit only where their interests happened to complement each other—as they had in February 1848. The demonstrators of 1849, Marx explained, gained only lackluster support and were routed by the bourgeois government. It is therefore doubly ironic that Marx's rhetoric in *The Civil War* contains an analogous form of appeal in the description of the alliance of the productive classes against their unproductive, degenerate oppressors.

Marx encouraged this cross-class alliance not because it was a fixed political objective but rather as a step toward a proletarian revolution. Where later Marxist politicians have sought to construct a cross-class coalition, they too have drawn on Marx's works on France to adopt the distinctions found in the intersecting structure. This is particularly evident in Europe during the interwar period, when individual Marxists such as Otto Bauer and August Thalheimer and then the Comintern began their attempts to forge a cross-class alliance against fascism.[27]

The fascists themselves, however, were peculiarly adept at appealing to the people. To some extent, they did so by using an analytic framework broadly similar to Marx's intersecting structure, through which they condemned financiers and "parasites" and appealed to "producers." Nonetheless, the fascist understanding of the majority of society was very different from that of Marx and later Marxists. This difference forms the subject of the next chapter, which resumes the earlier discussion of the shifting conceptions of the mob, by identifying how ideas of social Darwinism, the *élan vital*, and in particular, crowd psychology altered the meaning of both "mob" and "people" and related them to the concept of the masses.

NOTES

1. Karl Marx and Friedrich Engels, *The Communist Manifesto* (Harmondsworth: Penguin, 1967), p. 79.

2. *MECW*, vol. 10, p. 48.

3. Ibid., p. 49.

4. Ibid., p. 51.

5. Karl Marx, "The Civil War in France" (First Draft, Second Draft and Address of the General Council)," in *Karl Marx Friedrich Engels Gesamtausgabe*, vol. 1, part 22 (Berlin: Dietz Verlag, 1978), p. 139; see also pp. 104–5, 116.

6. For example, see Allin Cottrell, *Social Classes in Marxist Theory* (London: Routledge and Kegan Paul, 1984), pp. 44–58.

7. Karl Marx, *Capital*. vol. 1 (Chicago: Charles Kerr, 1912), p. 706.

8. Frank Bovenkerk, "The Rehabilitation of the Rabble; How and Why Marx and Engels Wrongly Depicted the Lumpenproletariat as a Reactionary Force," *Netherlands Journal of Sociology* 20 (April 1984), pp. 17–20.

9. See Stuart Hall, "The 'Political' and the 'Economic' in Marx's Theory of Classes," in *Class and Class Structure*, ed. Alan Hunt (London: Lawrence and Wishart, 1977).

10. *MECW*, vol. 10, p. 51. Emphasis in the original.

11. Ibid., p. 54. Emphasis in the original.

12. Ibid., vol. 11, p. 194.

13. Ibid., p. 139.

14. Marx, "The Civil War," p. 54.

15. *MECW* vol. 11, p. 191.

16. Ibid., pp. 182–83, 194–97.

17. Marx, "The Civil War," p. 63.

18. Ibid., p. 56; see also pp. 30–31, 41, 128.

19. Ibid., p. 143.

20. Ibid., pp. 138–139.

21. Ibid., pp. 115, 158.

22. Ibid., p. 59.

23. Philip E. Converse, "The Nature of Belief Systems in Mass Publics," in *Ideology and Discontent*, ed. David E. Apter (London: Macmillan, 1964); Giovanni Sartori, "Politics Ideology and Belief Systems," *American Political Science Review* 63 (1969): 398–411; Max Weber, " 'Objectivity' in Social Science and Social Policy," in *Max Weber on the Methodology of the Social Sciences*, ed. Edward Shils and Henry Finch (Glencoe, Ill.: Free Press, 1949).

24. See Ralph Miliband, *Marxism and Politics* (Oxford: Oxford University Press, 1977).

25. *MECW*, vol. 11, pp. 129–33.

26. Ibid., p. 133.

27. See Otto Bauer, "Fascism," in *Austro-Marxism*, eds. Tom Bottomore and Patrick Goode (Oxford: Clarendon Press, 1978); August Thalheimer, "On Fascism," trans. Judy Joseph, *Telos* 40 (Summer 1979): 109–22. Until the mid-1930s, the Communist International, which dominated the major communist parties in Europe, held that fascism was merely one manifestation of a wider reactionary political movement that encompassed the social democrats.

CHAPTER 4

The Emergence of the Crowd: Gustave Le Bon and the Fascist Concept of the Masses

The concept of the masses in fascist ideology is difficult to define because of the contradictions it entails. The masses were often described in terms of contempt, and yet mass support was actively sought. They could be led like sheep, and yet they had an instinct for the best political course to take.[1] They were stupid, and yet they perpetuated the highest characteristics of the nation or race.[2] The reasoning process through which these apparently inimical positions were integrated into fascist ideology was structured by three late nineteenth-century re-evaluations of the dichotomous concept of the masses as either the mob or the people. The first of these reassessments was undertaken by advocates of race inequality and by social Darwinists, the second by proponents of the *élan vital* and by defenders of mass violence, and the third by crowd theorists, including most notably Gustave Le Bon. Le Bon's crowd theory therefore was symptomatic of a much broader intellectual movement that prefigured the fascist concept of the masses, and the configuration of ideas that made up this concept can be traced to several overlapping sources. However, crowd theory was particularly significant for two reasons. The first was that the fascists' integration of differing strands of thought into their concept of the masses followed Le Bon's comprehensive incorporation of racist and violent political doctrines into crowd theory. The second was that the way in which Le Bon combined derivative ideas with the original insights of crowd theory was one that, despite its contradictions, gave the appearance of coherence. Crowd theory therefore allowed fascists to invoke incompatible views of the masses within a single, seemingly consistent, explanatory framework in a way that facilitated the plausibility and effectiveness of their propaganda.

Le Bon stands alongside Marx in his influence on radical ideologies in Europe. Like Marx, he incorporated established views of the distinction between "people" and "mob" with a novel perspective of the majority of the population, and like Marx, he developed an analytic framework that, because of its theoretical deficiencies, provided an effective basis for the development of popular ideological positions by radical politicians. Marx's method of shifting between class categories in his analysis is also found in Le Bon's changing views of the masses. But whereas for Marx, this technique was based on exploiting the similarities and differences between different class characteristics, Le Bon shifted between logically inimical views on the majority of the population. By using Le Bon's analytic framework in their own shifting views of the masses, fascists were able to combine elitist presuppositions with a broad popular appeal.

CROWD THEORY AND MASS PROPAGANDA

Benito Mussolini, who had "an intense interest in the psychology of the human masses—the crowd,"[3] singled out Le Bon's *Psychologie des foules* (The Crowd) as a work that had particularly impressed him.[4] The techniques of crowd manipulation Le Bon laid down are certainly suggestive of fascist propaganda. He said that

> an orator wishing to move a crowd must make an abusive use of violent affirmations. To exaggerate, to affirm, to resort to repetitions, and never to attempt to prove anything by reasoning are methods well known to speakers at public meetings.[5]

But, as this passage also suggests, such techniques were hardly the preserve of the fascists.

In order to appreciate that Le Bon's crowd theory did not merely describe fascist techniques but had a particular influence on fascist ideology, it can be noted that where the advocates of other political doctrines allowed such techniques to remain unmentioned, fascists openly incorporated the terminology of crowd psychology into their descriptions of the masses and how they could be manipulated. Several instances are found in Adolf Hitler's *Mein Kampf*.[6] Mass propaganda, Hitler wrote, "must confine itself to a few points and repeat them over and over."[7] It should appeal not to reason, but to the "primitive sentiments" and "emotional, always extreme, attitude of the great masses."[8] Le Bon had similarly described crowd sentiments as "very simple and very exaggerated. On this point, as on so many others, an individual in a crowd resembles primitive beings."[9]

The masses, Hitler argued, were like women: "so feminine by nature and attitude that sober reasoning determined their thoughts and actions far less than emotion and feeling."[10]

Le Bon had made the same comparison:

Among the special characteristics of crowds there are several—such as impulsiveness, irrationality, incapacity to reason, the absence of judgement and of the critical spirit, the exaggeration of the sentiments . . . —which are almost always observed in beings belonging to inferior forms of evolution—in women . . . for instance.[11]

Hitler added that just as a woman "would rather bow to a strong man than dominate a weakling, . . . the masses would love a commander more than a petitioner and feel inwardly more satisfied by a doctrine, tolerating no other beside itself, than by the granting of liberalistic freedom."[12] This argument also followed from Le Bon:

Authoritativeness and intolerance are sentiments of which crowds have a very clear notion. . . . Crowds exhibit a docile respect for force but are slightly impressed by kindness, which for them is scarcely other than a form of weakness. Their sympathies have never been bestowed on easy-going masters, but on tyrants. . . . A crowd is always ready to revolt against a feeble and to bow down servilely before a strong authority.[13]

Similar views were expressed by Mussolini, who among other things, said: "The crowd loves strong men. The crowd is like a woman."[14]

Despite the evidence that the terms fascists used to describe the masses were influenced by crowd theory, the fascist concept of the masses might appear to derive from a much earlier source. Fascists outlined propaganda techniques that assumed the masses to be highly emotional and of limited intelligence.[15] These assumptions are very similar to the long-established elite view of the masses as the *mobile vulgus*, the turbulent common people. Given this similarity, and given that the techniques described by crowd theorists were already used, if not admitted to, by other political orators, it might be concluded that the only role Le Bon and other crowd theorists had in the development of fascism was a Machiavellian one: They provided fascists with an understanding of the masses that was already known to elitist politicians who engaged in populist rhetoric.[16]

The comparison between the qualities imputed to the masses and the idea of the *mobile vulgus*, however, refers to only part of the concept of the masses that fascists found in crowd theory. The novelty of this concept, considered as a whole, was that it combined the idea of the masses as emotive and irrational with that of the "mass soul," the idea that the masses somehow embodied the sentiments, interests, and beliefs that would shape the destiny of a nation or race.[17] To understand the reasoning process through which these ideas were combined, it is necessary to examine a two-stage conceptual transformation undertaken by crowd theorists. The first stage was the shift from the idea of the mob to that of the crowd; the second was a shift from the idea of the crowd to that of the masses.

FROM MOB TO CROWD

In Chapter 1, we have seen that around the time of the French Revolution, there developed the widespread idea that crowds engaged in hostile collective action could be distinguished from the population at large. The majority of society were defined not as the volatile, fractious *mobile vulgus*, but as being stable and industrious—as the people. From such a perspective, the people could be contrasted with the shiftless, lazy, floating population of thieves and vagabonds who were said to make up demonstrating crowds.

It was this latter group that gained the appellation "mob." Although "mob" was an abbreviation of *mobile vulgus*, the term increasingly came to be used to refer not to the low, unstable majority of the population, but rather to a vicious, unproductive minority, a "dangerous class" that was distinct from the laboring classes. This etymological shift in the meaning of the mob from majority to minority was symptomatic of the broader process of elite accommodation to the extension of the franchise and to mass involvement in politics. By the late nineteenth century, violent crowd protests, riots, and rebellions were generally attributed to this latter type of mob.

This was the background to the publication, in 1891, of Scipio Sighele's *La Folla delinquenta* (The Criminal Crowd). This was not the first description of crowd behavior, although it was the first book in which the subject was discussed systematically.[18] The previous year, Gabriel Tarde had published *La Philosophie panale*. Embedded in Tarde's analysis of the conditions in the big cities that engendered crime was a short speculative passage on the power of suggestion and imitation in determining mob behavior.[19] Sighele took up this argument.[20] He contended that it was necessary to separate people's behavior in crowds from their behavior as individuals or distinct social groups. The markedly similar behavior exhibited by heterogeneous crowds composed of people of different sex, ages, moral sense, and degree of culture, Sighele reasoned, could not be attributed to the common social backgrounds of their members.[21] This argument was the first step in the transition from the mob to the crowd, as the identification of common forms of crowd behavior, carried to its furthest extent, undermined the association drawn between violent collective action and an unproductive substratum of the population. Sighele, however, shrank from such a conclusion.

Sighele's retreat from the deductive consequences of his argument is made evident in his discussion of the composition and action of crowds in the French Revolution. After condemning the brutality of crowd outrages, Sighele asked:

> But was it really just the influence of numbers and the sudden awakening of homicidal instincts which pushed [the people] to the point of committing unparalleled excesses? Was it really the people, honest workers and peasants, who suddenly became monsters of perversity?[22]

Sighele answered this rhetorical question with another: Was it not true that the violent crowds of the French Revolution were composed of the lowest strata of society—brigands, vagabonds, adventurers, those who lived without working?[23] Was it not recognized that in unsettled times, these people emerged from their taverns and evil dwellings in the same way that "when one agitates the water of a pond, all the mud at the bottom rises to the surface?"[24] This was a retreat to the type of imagery of the mob that preceded crowd theory, imagery which referred to it as the "scum" that floated on society or the "deep mephitic mud" beneath it.

When Le Bon's *Psychologie des foules* appeared, to instant success, in 1895, Sighele complained of plagiarism.[25] It was, however, Le Bon who separated crowd behavior, even in its most extreme manifestations, from the behavior of individual criminals, and who disputed the assumption that violent crowds were composed of an unproductive, dangerous rabble. It was Le Bon, therefore, who took the second, decisive step in the conceptual shift from the mob to the crowd.[26]

Le Bon advanced his argument by referring to Hippolyte Taine's account of the September massacres of 1791 in a way that subtly transformed Taine's analysis. Taine was perhaps the most influential nineteenth-century historian to identify popular participation in the French Revolution with the mob; in every act of the revolution, Taine saw the mass involvement of a minority of unemployed vagabonds, criminals, adventurers, and so on. The majority of society was indicted not for its participation in the revolution but for its apathy:

> The slime, on rising from the bottom has become the surface, and given its color to the stream; but the human stream . . . remains about the same as it was before. . . . To the great majority, even in revolutionary times, private life . . . leaves but an insignificant corner for public affairs.[27]

Taine's account of the massacres, however, was atypical in that he supplemented his main thesis to argue that not only had a mob of "former soldiers or old bandits, deserters, bohemians, and bullies of all lands and from every source"[28] participated in the killings, but so had mainstream Parisians. Seizing on the latter, Le Bon down played the role of the former. Where Taine had indicated that the mob formed a considerable proportion of the murderers, Le Bon described them as an insignificant exception to the "shopkeepers and artisans of every trade" who engaged in the massacres.[29]

The shift in emphasis over who the murderers were was followed by a reinterpretation of their psychology. Taine implicitly described a gradual descent into bestiality by the killers. Their initial reluctance to commit murder shifted by degrees to an enthusiasm for the prolonged torture of their victims; similarly, their initial honesty in not stealing even from those they killed degenerated into a general licence to commit robbery.[30] Le Bon, however, saw the behavior of the murderers as a constant; they underwent an instant transformation to crowd psychology.

In describing this psychology, Le Bon selectively identified patterns of behavior Taine had used to illustrate the dynamic stages in the degeneration into barbarism as characteristic of the crowd all the way through the massacre. Two of these behavior traits were taken from the opposite ends of Taine's dynamic: While the killers had behaved with a ferocious brutality throughout, they had also been consistently scrupulous in handing over the property of the victims to the revolutionary committees.[31] The significance of this juxtaposition was that it could be used to support Le Bon's conclusion that not only were crowds generally deemed to be "criminal" in fact likely to be composed of the population at large, but also that their actions did not spring from antisocial propensities or from the moral limitations of the classes from which they were drawn. The actions of such crowds, Le Bon said, were rather the result of their extreme passions combined with their belief in the suggestion that the expression of these passions served a high moral purpose.[32]

FROM CROWD TO MASS

The re-evaluation of the composition and motives of crowds provided the background to a further shift in the interpretation of violent collective action. This shift compounded the idea that crowd behavior occurred only under certain conditions with the idea that such behavior was characteristic of the masses.

In his analysis of Robert Michels's shift from being a supporter of socialism to a supporter of fascism, David Beetham suggests that Michels's work exhibited a "slippage" between the concepts of the crowd and the masses that typified much social science writing in the early twentieth century.[33] This "slippage," Beetham argues, took place in three steps.[34] The first step was to broaden the idea of the crowd as a large gathering to mean any form of combination in which individuals shared a common reference point—such as a newspaper—without being within physical proximity to each other. The second step was to see the behavior of such a group as indicative of the general psychological state of the majority of the population. The third step was to equate this majority with the masses. (The two terms are not synonymous. The majority of a population might include elites, but the masses are invariably contrasted with elite groups.)

All of these steps are found in the work of crowd theorists. The shift from the first to the second step was justified by defining the crowd in psychological rather than physical terms.[35] At this point, crowd theorists branched out in two directions. They identified the effects of crowd psychology in distinct social groups, described as sects or homogeneous crowds.[36] However, they also went from the second to the third step in identifying the crowd with the masses. This shift often went unexamined as, like "mob," the term "mass" and its cognates already evoked the idea of a crowd. However, it was sometimes justified by the premise that there was an inverse relationship between levels of education or intelligence and susceptibility to crowd behavior.[37]

To identify the reasoning process fascists derived from crowd theory, however, it is necessary to analyze the second step not simply as part of a linear sequence of shifting concepts, but rather as compounding two ideas of the type of behavior exhibited by crowds: the idea that such behavior was atavistic and the idea that it was collective. Although these ideas were distinct, they could be linked through the analogous process of regression. The idea that the crowd regressed to a savage state was combined with the idea that it exhibited a regression to collective societal traits.

The barbarous behavior of crowds was condemned by most crowd theorists in conventional moral terms. From a radical right-wing perspective, however, the idea that the crowd expressed certain essential national or racial characteristics could be seen as a positive feature of its behavior. It was from this ideological viewpoint that the atavistic and collective components of crowd behavior became compounded. This was done not by evaluating crowd behavior in terms of a trade-off between its savagery and its collectivism, but by seeing in its savagery the affirmation of its collective national or racial characteristics. This line of reasoning, which saw the masses as expressing their "soul" through violent crowd behavior, was taken up by the fascists. At the same time, fascists retained the idea, implicit in the notion of regression, that such behavior denoted the inferiority of the masses as against the elite. It was this theoretically syncretic yet ideologically effective view of the masses that could be found in the form of crowd theory popularized by Le Bon.

THE AMBIGUITY OF CROWD THEORY

Nineteenth-century apologists for mass violence had typically justified it as the emancipatory struggle of an oppressed group. For example, Jules Michelet, in contrast to Taine, had identified the crowd in the French Revolution as the people rather than as the mob. The revolutionary violence of the people was understated and excused by the emphasis Michelet placed on the centuries of atrocities committed under the Ancien

Regime.[38] Although similar justifications for mass violence were made by fascists, the novelty of the fascist doctrine was that mass violence was identified not simply as a reaction against oppression and a means of realizing external aspirations but was also seen as an inherent quality of the people, one that allowed them to realize their intrinsic characteristics.

The fascist condemnation of parliamentarism provides an example. Parliamentary democracy was said by fascists to allow "a mob of the lowest scoundrels" to live off producers: "The fruit of the honest work of other folk has been stolen by those who themselves never worked."[39] But parliamentarians were contrasted with the people not only through being unproductive, but also for engaging in reasoned argument rather than violent action.[40]

The justification for violence as natural and intrinsic bore some resemblance to the arguments made by Friedrich Nietzsche, although Nietzsche's endorsement of the violence of the "strong" toward the masses was, in effect, extended to the masses.[41] The fascist re-evaluation of mass violence, therefore, had more similarities with the views of the populist right in late nineteenth-century France,[42] as well as with radical left-wing justifications of violence.[43] Considered in terms of overall structure, however, it was Le Bon's theory of the crowd that, among late nineteenth-century writings, corresponded most closely to fascist ideology. This was not because Le Bon developed a more extensive justification of mass violence than other writers but because of the ambiguous context in which he viewed mass violence and other forms of mass action.

The ambiguity of Le Bon's attitude toward the crowd, and hence the masses, was not expressed through equivocation but by contradictory affirmations. He wrote, for example, that "civilizations as yet have only been created and directed by a small intellectual aristocracy, never by crowds, crowds are only powerful for destruction."[44] This appears to be conclusive, until we read:

> We should not complain too much that crowds are . . . guided by unconscious reasoning. Had they, in certain cases, reasoned and consulted their immediate interests, it is possible that no civilization would have grown up on our planet, and humanity would have had no history.[45]

Le Bon's contradictory views on the crowd extended to his evaluation of their behavior. This behavior was described as both debased and heroic: "By the mere fact that he forms part of an organised crowd, a man descends several rungs in the ladder of civilization. . . . He possesses the spontaneity, the violence, the ferocity, and also the enthusiasm and heroism of primitive beings."[46] This combination of brutal and noble impulses meant that "a crowd may be guilty of murder, incendiarism, and every kind of crime, but it is also capable of very lofty acts of devotion, sacrifice, and disinterestedness."[47]

These two forms of behavior became one when crowd violence was directed at the realization of some "real or chimerical ideal."[48] Such an ideal, however, was not only an external objective but was also the expression of the essential nature of the crowd that pursued it. In revising Taine's interpretation of the French Revolution, therefore, Le Bon argued that in describing the revolutionaries as "a horde of epileptic savages abandoning themselves without restraint to their instincts," Taine had not realized that, for all its violence, such an event expressed the crowd's "soul."[49]

Le Bon's ambiguous evaluation of crowd behavior had an underlying contradiction as a result of the way in which he had superimposed crowd theory on two established ideas. These ideas were: first, that the social structure within a society resulted from natural individual inequalities; second, that the differences between societies and their relations with each other could be explained by societal inequalities. Le Bon attributed both types of inequality to race, and it was from this social-Darwinist perspective that he ranked the crowd, or masses, in two separate hierarchies. Within a society, the masses were seen as being racially inferior to the elite. Between societies, however, the European masses (i.e., the Aryan masses) were seen by Le Bon as a superior race.[50] These two opposing interpretations of the comparative racial position of the masses corresponded with the two forms of regressive crowd behavior: atavism and collectivism. Considered within a society, the regression to savagery accentuated the distinction between the racial development of the masses and the elite. But if regressive behavior was considered between societies, the obliteration of individual distinctions for underlying collective traits could be identified with the expression of superior racial characteristics. By compounding these regressive characteristics, however, either view of the racial level of the masses could be linked to both forms of crowd behavior.

A second contradiction was Le Bon's dual conception of mass action as both objective and subjective. On the one hand, the propensity of crowds to act on the basis of their emotions rather than on reason was seen as making them susceptible to manipulation. On the other hand, this same propensity for emotional over reasoned behavior was seen as explaining the objective basis of their actions in their instinctive expression of collective race characteristics. Taken together, these two contradictions were, if not logical, nonetheless embracive: They provided a framework into which any type of mass action could be fit.

The significance of this theoretical structure to fascists was the way in which it allowed them to combine an abstract extremism with a substantive doctrine of the people. Both qualities have been interpreted as fundamental to fascist ideology. Marxist and other analysts of the "petit bourgeois" appeal of fascism have stressed its mass appeal to a nation of "producers"—one method of identifying the people—rather than to workers. Mass society theorists have focused on the fanaticism and violence with which fascist doctrine was pursued. The link between these two aspects of fascist ideology in crowd theory, however, has received little attention from either perspective, and it is instructive to briefly consider why.

The Marxist activists who first developed the petit bourgeois thesis of fascism were concerned, at both a theoretical and a practical level, to separate fascist supporters from the working class.[51] But if crowd techniques were an effective element of fascist ideology, the natural conclusion was that the appeal of fascism cut across classes. Crowd psychology called into question the theory that class interests determined mass action, and socialists could not "*on pain of self-betrayal* appeal like fascism to the lower instincts of crowds."[52] To this could be added that if socialists did attempt to appeal to the masses in this way, they could not admit to it without compromising their vision of the crowd event par excellence: the Revolution.

Mass society theorists had a different reason to neglect the connection established by Le Bon. Considerably indebted to crowd theory for their analysis of fascism's success,[53] they nonetheless divested it of the irrationalist idea that crowd behavior exhibited the spirit of a nation, race, or people. In doing so, however, they focused on the fascist use of crowd techniques to appeal to "atomized, isolated individuals,"[54] to the exclusion of the substantive doctrine of the people to which these techniques were linked.

CROWD THEORY AND FASCIST IDEOLOGY

The links between abstract extremism and the substantive appeal to the people are apparent in the anti-socialist and anti-Semitic elements of

fascist ideology. Socialists and Jews were long-standing objects of enmity
in the eyes of the right. Fascist propaganda used the contradictory analysis
of the masses found in crowd theory to promote this established antipathy.
It did so by combining implicit techniques of mass appeal with a series of
explicit contrasts between socialists, Jews, and their supporters on the one
hand, and fascists and their supporters on the other.

The development of the fascist ideology of anti-socialism was structured by the attempt to gain mass support in the face of the popularity of
the socialist parties. Acknowledging the strength of support for socialism,
the fascists argued that it was due to the use of crowd techniques by its
leaders.[55] It was from the basis of this deduction that the contradictory
views of the masses found in fascist anti-socialism began to appear. It
has been seen that Hitler and Mussolini had a close interest in techniques
of crowd manipulation. It might be concluded, therefore, that they saw
themselves as appealing to the masses using the same methods as the
socialists. However, the fascist leaders themselves depicted the effect of
their techniques upon the masses as being very different from those of
the socialists.

The first difference, fascists claimed, was that where their use of
crowd psychology was directed at the mass soul, socialists used crowd
psychology to appeal to the gullibility of the masses and exploit their
susceptibility to being manipulated.[56] This was an example of fascists'
use of the ambiguous evaluation of the masses as both objective and
subjective. It was a distinction that the fascists combined with the second
ambiguity: the evaluation of the masses as inferior and as superior. The
mass supporters of socialism were characterized as being inferior;
they were stupid,[57] and their behavior was savage and degenerate.[58]
While this description was consistent with the broader characterization
of the masses as belonging to "the mob of the simple or credulous,"[59]
it contrasted completely with the way in which the active supporters
of fascism were depicted. This group was said to be an elite, one that
exemplified the highest qualities of the nation or race. This concept of
the membership of fascist movements might therefore seem simply to be
separate from the fascist concept of the masses, were it not for the fact
that the methods that were used to attract active members—the prospect
of violence, the extreme propaganda[60]—were the same crowd techniques
with which socialists were said to appeal to the most primitive instincts
of the most inferior part of the population.

The contradiction between these two views of the masses was accentuated by the link fascists made between their opposition to the socialists

and their own quest for mass support. The extreme physical and rhetorical violence with which socialists were attacked by fascists was itself a technique of appealing to the crowd, but one that, insofar as it succeeded, was seen as having reached the "soul of the people."[61]

In *The Psychology of Socialism*, Le Bon suggested that socialism might achieve its destiny despite its political deficiencies because it inspired fanatical faith and was poised to replace a civilization in decline. It was, however, typical of Le Bon that he refuted this suggestion in the same work. Thus, Le Bon juxtaposed the malleability of the masses with their unchanging spiritual essence to explain both that socialism would triumph through using crowd techniques and that it would fail and be repudiated by the soul of the masses. Socialists, Le Bon wrote,

> are skilled in the art of persuasion. . . . They know that the crowd has a horror of doubt; that they knew none but extreme sentiments, energetic affirmation, energetic denial, intense love, or violent hatred; and they know how to evolve these sentiments and how to develop them.[62]

Yet this argument was followed by an opposite one:

> The agitations of the crowd have their being above the immutable depths that the movements of the surface do not reach; and this depth consists of those hereditary instincts whose sum is the soul of the nation. . . . To these hereditary instincts the crowd always returns. . . . The Socialists imagine that they will easily carry the masses with them. They are wrong. . . . They will find among the masses not their allies but their most implacable enemies.[63]

The contradictory structure on which Le Bon built this argument was used by the fascists in their distinction between socialist supporters and their own adherents. The shallow socialist appeal to the crowd was contrasted with the fascists' appeal to the mass soul, while the techniques fascists used to gain mass support were indistinguishable from those they attributed to the socialists. This form of argument allowed fascists to claim that it was they and not the socialists who embodied the true new faith that would replace the decadent democracies.[64]

The anti-Semitic ideology that characterized fascist movements outside Italy was similar to and often inseparable from their anti-socialist doctrines.[65] Like the socialists, Jews were seen as using crowd techniques to fool the masses and, in fact, socialism itself was generally attributed to the supposed Jewish conspiracy. Le Bon was not noticeably anti-Semitic. Although his discussions on Jews depended on racist presuppositions, he did not single out their malign intentions. The only influence of Le Bon's crowd theory on this aspect of fascism is, therefore, an indirect one. Le Bon provided not an anti-Semitic depiction of the Jews but a structure in which such a depiction could be placed. His re-evaluation of the nineteenth-century categories of mob and people and his incorporation of doctrines of race and violence into crowd theory provided the framework with which violent mass hostility to the Jews could be defined in positive terms. The ambiguous concept of the crowd, with its connotations of inferiority and superiority, subjectivity and objectivity, acted as the connecting point or locus to an ideology that switched from *mobile vulgus*, to mob, to people. Through this reasoning process, the anti-Semitic ideology of fascism was fashioned to appeal to the soul of the people. It appealed to the masses to take extreme, violent anti-Semitic action to safeguard their common interests as producers and thus fulfill their racial destiny.

The fascists' most widely disseminated work of anti-Semitic propaganda, the *Protocols of the Learned Elders of Zion*, made frequent reference to mass manipulation by Jews. Little of this depiction can be attributed to crowd theory because the source of much of the forged *Protocols*, Maurice Joly's *Dialogues in Hell Between Machiavelli and Montesquieu*, predates publication of *Psychologie des foules* by about thirty years.[66] However, the *Protocols*, in its final form, was probably written in Paris in 1897 or 1898, two or three years after Le Bon's book came out.[67] This may help to explain the shift in emphasis between the *Dialogues*, in which "Machiavelli" argues for mass repression, and the *Protocols*, which has the Jews advocating mass manipulation. In Joly's work, Machiavelli asks: "Is it possible to conduct by pure reason violent masses which are moved only by sentiment, passion, and prejudice?"[68]

But where in the *Dialogues* this rhetorical question is used to justify the violent battle against these masses, "the enemies within,"[69] in the *Protocols*, the same qualities signified how the masses might be used as tools to gain power in the state.[70] Thus, in the *Dialogues*, the question of controlling the masses is one "less of suppressing their political instincts than of *wiping them out*,"[71] while in the parallel passage in the *Protocols*, we read: "It is more important to use burning passions for our cause than to extinguish them."[72]

Despite this shift, it might be questioned whether the concept of the masses found in the *Protocols* differs significantly from the *mobile vulgus*.

As has been seen, the novelty and significance of crowd theory lay not simply in that it detailed techniques of mass manipulation for political purposes, but also in that it developed, altered, and compounded the dichotomous ideas of the people and the mob. But this is not evident in the *Protocols*, as the masses are characterized in a way that is almost completely one-sided: "The crowd is a barbarian."[73]

The concept of the masses as the people, however, was present not in what was written within the text but in the unstated effect that the forgery was intended to have. The *Protocols* were designed to generate mass hostility toward the Jews, to provoke pogroms. It was this form of mass action that was seen as being undertaken not by "the stupid mob"[74] but by the people, and it was in this context that a book concocted by the tsar's secret police could later be exploited by fascists.

The value of the *Protocols* was that it ostensibly connected the Jews with the masses *qua mobile vulgus*, while implicitly assuming that this would encourage the masses *qua* people to be anti-Semitic. These two contradictory views of the masses were developed in two directions. One direction was to interpret violent mass hostility to the Jews as an expression of the essence of the people. Alexander Cuza's article, "The Science of Anti-Semitism," provides an example of this type of argument.[75] Cuza said that those who had been "Judaized" saw in attacks against Jews "only a savagery, a blind manifestation of brutal instincts, vestiges of prehistoric times."[76] Cuza attacked this conventional and humanitarian idea that anti-Semitic violence was, in effect, the work of a mob.[77] He did so, however, not by denying that such violence displayed an instinctive savagery, but rather by positively redefining it as the "energy" of the people. Cuza's "scientific" contribution to the expression of such energy lay in "enlightening further the consciousness of people, fully satisfying their instinct and its violent eruptions thus legitimized by revealing their cause—the parasitism of the Jews."[78] Thus, Cuza dismissed the charge that anti-Semitism encouraged " 'the stirring of bestial instincts in popular masses,' "[79] by describing the violent actions of such crowds as embodying national and racial traits and displaying a healthy brutality. This allowed the conclusion that extreme anti-Semitic propaganda appealed not to the worst in people but to the best in them.

The association between the Jews and the *mobile vulgus* developed in a more ambiguous direction to serve more than one ideological function. At one level, the anti-democratic sentiments on which the association was based, the idea that "modern plebian Jews . . . have an affinity with the mob,"[80] supported fascists in their elitism, their condemnation of parliamentarism, and the degenerate stigma they attached to their socialist opponents. At another level, however, the mass appeal of fascism to the people relied on the implication that the link between Jews and the mob indicated that they were an unproductive minority.

Cuza's description of the Jews as "parasites" followed established anti-Semitic usage. The term meant first that Jews were foreign to the body of a nation, and second, that they were unproductive, lacked "a definite attitude towards the concept of work,"[81] and had "an evident inclination . . . to seize upon the production of others without producing themselves."[82] This depiction of the Jews had certain similarities to the concept of the mob as an unproductive minority, and it had not taken the advent of fascism for these two groups to be linked together in ideologies that sought a mass appeal. This link, somewhat indirect, has been mentioned in the discussion of Arendt's *Origins of Totalitarianism* in the Introduction to this book. If society was imagined as having two extremes, with the mob at the lower end and the people in the middle, the mob was associated with a class containing financiers, which, while it lay at the opposite end of this social scale, was alleged to share a common degeneracy and unwillingness to produce with the mob. These financiers in turn, could be described—as they were by Marx—as "Bourse Jews," or "The Jews of Finance."[83] Fascists were able to consolidate this link between the mob and the Jews through the separation of crowd violence from the mob found in Le Bon's crowd theory. Not only were the Jews parasites on the productiveness of the people, but the attacks on Jews by crowds, the apparent epitome of mob violence, could be categorized not as attacks by the mob, but rather as attacks on the mob by the people.[84]

VIOLENCE AND THE PEOPLE

The masses described by Le Bon altered the concepts of people and mob by compounding social Darwinism and the espousal of violence with contradictory explanations of crowd regression. Le Bon suggested that it was unnecessary to use reason in techniques of mass propaganda, and his own analysis embodied substantial contradictions. Fascists were able to use the contradictory theoretical framework developed by Le Bon both to characterize their mass supporters and to identify their mass opponents. This process involved the identification of opponents as inferior or manipulated, while supporters were described as expressing a higher purpose and embodying the mass soul.

The fascist concept of the masses therefore retained the established distinctions between people and mob, while at the same time it adapted and added to the terms of this dichotomy. The structural basis for these changes was found in Le Bon's shift from the mob to the crowd to the masses. The crowd theory of Le Bon provided not a deductive sequence of ideas leading to inevitable conclusions, but rather a parallel structure of ambiguous and logically incompatible ideas that allowed shifting meanings to be attached to the idea of the crowd. Fascists used the contradictory ideas that Le Bon had developed at a theoretical level to combine their doctrinal views with their methods of appealing for mass support. They deliberately characterized their opponents in extreme terms as a means of attracting supporters, added racial dimensions to their depiction of the masses, and tied both of these ideas to an endorsement of emotive, violent, and intolerant political behavior. Thus, the violence of the mob became redefined as the energy of the people. The way to reach this energy was by appealing to crowd psychology, and to make such an appeal, opponents were identified with the mob.

NOTES

1. Emil Ludwig, *Talks with Mussolini*, trans. Eden and Cedar Paul (Boston: Little Brown and Co., 1933), pp. 120, 127; Benito Mussolini, *My Autobiography* (New York: Charles Scribner's Sons, 1928), p. 191.

2. Adolf Hitler, *Mein Kampf*, trans. Ralph Manheim (London: Hutchinson, 1969), pp. 165, 219–20, 306–7.

3. Mussolini, *My Autobiography*, p. 11.

4. Ibid., p. 25. Other references by Mussolini to Le Bon, and the correspondence between them, are described in Robert A. Nye, *The Origins of Crowd Psychology: Gustave Le Bon and the Crisis of Mass Democracy in the Third Republic* (London: Sage, 1975), p. 178.

5. Le Bon, *The Crowd*, p. 57.

6. Parallels between *Mein Kampf* and *The Crowd* are discussed in Alfred Stein, "Adolf Hitler und Gustave Le Bon," *Geschichte in Wissenschaft und Unterricht* 6 (1955): 362–68; Nye, *The Origins of Crowd Psychology*, p. 179.

7. Hitler, *Mein Kampf*, p. 168.

8. Ibid., pp. 167, 168.

9. Le Bon, *The Crowd*, p. 56.

10. Hitler, *Mein Kampf*, p. 167.

11. Le Bon, *The Crowd*, p. 40.

12. Hitler, *Mein Kampf*, p. 39.

13. Le Bon, *The Crowd*, p. 61.

14. Ludwig, *Talks with Mussolini*, p. 62.

15. Hitler, *Mein Kampf*, pp. 164–65.

16. Hence, crowd theory could be said to be Machiavellian not only in the sense of teaching an elite group—the fascist leaders—to manipulate the masses, but also in the sense of Rousseau and Gramsci: teaching those outside the power structure what those within already knew. See Jean-Jacques Rousseau, *The Social Contract*, trans. G.D.H.Cole (London: J. M. Dent and Sons, 1973), p. 221; Antonio Gramsci, *The Modern Prince* (New York: International Publishers, 1957), pp. 141–42.

17. In Le Bon's *The Psychology of Peoples* (New York: G. E. Stechert, 1912), these characteristics were "the three fundamental bases of the soul of a people" (p. 13). Le Bon compounded the meaning of "people" with "race." Despite the title of the work, he described its object as being "to describe the psychological characteristics which constitute the soul of races" (p. xvii). Race, in its turn was compounded with "nation": The "aggregate of psychological elements observable in all individuals of a race constitutes what may rightly be called the national character" (p. 6).

18. Several nineteenth-century literary figures described crowd behavior, including Edmond Goncourt, *Journal des Goncourt 1870–71* (Paris: Bibliothèque Charpentier, 1890), pp. 9–10, 48–49, 104–6; Guy de Maupassant, *Afloat*, trans. Laura Ensor (London: George Routledge and Sons, 1889), pp. 158–64; Emile Zola, *Germinal*, ed. Ernest Alfred Vizetelly (London: Chatto and Windus, 1901), pp. 234–46. All three works were mentioned as sources by Sighele.

19. Gabriel Tarde, *Penal Philosophy*, trans. Rapelje Howell (Boston: Little Brown and Co., 1912), pp. 322–26. Tarde's *The Laws of Imitation*, trans. Elsie Clews Parsons (London: Henry Holt, 1903; first publ. 1890), pp. 74–88, contained a general discussion of "*unconscious* imitation" by members of social groups.

20. The influence of Tarde on Sighele's work is discussed in Robert L. Geiger, "Democracy and the Crowd: The Social History of an Idea in France and Italy, 1890–1914," *Societas* 7 (1977): 47–71.

21. Sighele, *La Foule criminelle: essai de psychologie collective* (Paris: Felix Alcan, 1901), p. 21. This is a translation of the second edition of *La Folla Delinquenta*.

22. Sighele, *La Foule criminelle*, p. 92.

23. Ibid., pp. 92–95.

24. Ibid., p. 92. Sighele may have identified crowd behavior with criminals because of the influence of Italian criminology. See Robert E. Park, *The Crowd and the Public*, trans. Charlotte Elsner (Chicago: University of Chicago Press, 1972), pp. 6–7.

25. Sighele, *La Foule criminelle*, p. i.

26. Sighele repudiated Le Bon's argument in *La Foule criminelle*, pp. 138–41. Le Bon explicitly distinguished himself from Sighele in *The Psychology*

of Socialism (New York: Macmillan, 1899), p. 100, n. 1. A chapter in *The Crowd*, "Crowds termed criminal crowds," pp. 183–89, was implicitly directed against Sighele.

27. Hippolyte Adolphe Taine, *The Origins of Contemporary France, The French Revolution*, 2 vols., trans. John Durand (New York: Henry Holt, 1896), vol. 2, p. 188.

28. Ibid., vol. 2, p. 219.

29. Le Bon, *The Crowd*, p. 185.

30. Taine, *The French Revolution*, vol. 2, pp. 219–31.

31. Le Bon, *The Crowd*, pp. 65, 187–88.

32. Ibid., pp. 185–89.

33. Beetham, "From Socialism to Fascism in the Work of Robert Michels. II: The Fascist Ideologue," *Political Studies* 25 (1977): 161–81.

34. Ibid., p. 175.

35. Le Bon, *The Crowd*, pp. 25–26.

36. Scipio Sighele wrote of sects in *Psychologie des sectes*, trans. Louis Brandin (Paris: V. Giard and E. Briere, 1898). Le Bon distinguished between heterogeneous and homogeneous crowds in *The Crowd*, p. 27.

37. Gabriel Tarde, *L'Opinion et la foule* (Paris: Felix Alcan, 1904), p. 7; Park, *The Crowd and the Public*, p. 80; Everett Dean Martin, *The Behavior of Crowds* (New York: Harper and Brothers, 1920), pp. 281–303.

38. Jules Michelet, *History of the French Revolution*, trans. Charles Cocks, ed. Gordon Wright (Chicago: University of Chicago Press, 1967).

39. Adolf Hitler, *The Speeches of Adolf Hitler April 1922–August 1939*, 2 vols., trans. Norman H. Baynes (New York: Howard Ferlig, 1969), vol. 1, p. 79.

40. For example, see Oswald Mosley, *Fascism: 100 Questions* (London: British Union of Fascists, 1936), p. 9; *The Greater Britain* (London: BUF, 1934), pp. 50, 53.

41. Friedrich Nietzsche, *The Will to Power*, trans. Walter Kaufmann and R. J. Hollingdale (New York: Random House, 1968), pp. 61–62; *The Genealogy of Morals*, trans. Horace B. Samuel (New York: Russell and Russell, 1964), pp. 38–43.

42. Such views were exemplified in the works of Barrès. See Maurice Barès, *Les Deracinés* (Paris: Librarie Plon, 1922); Robert Soucy, *Fascism in France: The Case of Maurice Barrès* (Berkeley: University of California Press, 1972); Zeev Sternhell, "Irrationalism and Violence in the French Radical Right: The Case of Maurice Barrès," in Philip P. Wiener and John Fisher, eds., *Violence and Aggression in the History of Ideas* (New Brunswick, N.J.: Rutgers University Press, 1974), pp. 79–98.

43. Sorel's views on violence were of particular significance. See Georges Sorel, *Reflections on Violence*, trans. T. E. Hulme (London: George Allen and Unwin, 1915); Wilfried Rohrich, "George Sorel and the Myth of Violence," in

Wolfgang J. Mommsen and Gerhard Hirschfeld, eds., *Social Protest, Violence and Terror in Nineteenth- and Twentieth-Century Europe* (London: Macmillan, 1982), pp. 246–56; Jack J. Roth, *The Cult of Violence: Sorel and the Sorelians* (Berkeley: University of California Press, 1980); Nye, *The Origins of Crowd Psychology*, pp. 101–13.

44. Le Bon, *The Crowd*, p. 19. William Kornkhauser quotes this passage in support of his definition of Le Bon as an aristocratic critic of mass society, in *The Politics of Mass Society* (Glencoe, Ill.: The Free Press, 1959). p. 29.

45. Le Bon, *The Crowd*, p. 66. See also *The Psychology of Peoples*, pp. 175–76.

46. Le Bon, *The Crowd*, p. 36.

47. Ibid., p. 64.

48. Ibid., p. 66.

49. Ibid., pp. 86–87.

50. Le Bon, *Psychology of Peoples*, pp. 26–27, 40, 42–43, 51, 129, 175–76, 199–200.

51. The theory of petit bourgeois support for fascism had been developed by socialist opponents to Mussolini by the early 1920s. See *Marxists in Face of Fascism*, ed. David Beetham (Manchester: Manchester University Press, 1983); Antonio Gramsci, *Selections from Political Writings 1921–1926*, trans. Quintin Hoare (New York: International Publishers, 1978).

52. Daniel Guerin, *Fascism and Big Business*, trans. Frances and Mason Merrill (New York: Pioneer Publishers, 1939), p. 67.

53. Le Bon's work is cited by several mass society theorists. See Kornhauser, *The Politics*, pp. 22–30; Emil Lederer, *State of the Masses* (New York: W. W. Norton, 1940), pp. 227–29; Sigmund Neumann, *Permanent Revolution* (New York: Frederick Praeger, 1965), p. 113; Joseph Schumpeter, *Capitalism, Socialism and Democracy* (New York: Harper and Row, 1950), pp 256–57.

54. Hannah Arendt, *The Origins of Totalitarianism*, 3rd ed. (New York: Harcourt, Brace and World, 1966), p. 323.

55. Hitler, *Mein Kampf*, pp. 58–59, 161, 311.

56. Mussolini, *My Autobiography*, p. 112.

57. Hitler, *Mein Kampf*, p. 294.

58. Mussolini, *My Autobiography*, p. 133.

59. Hitler, *Mein Kampf*, p. 220.

60. Mussolini, *My Autobiography*, pp. 124–25; Hitler, *Mein Kampf*, pp. 527–34.

61. Hitler, *Mein Kampf*, p. 307.

62. Le Bon, *Psychology of Socialism*, p. 90.

63. Ibid., p. 103.

64. Hitler, *Mein Kampf*, pp. 339–46.

65. Anti-Semitic laws were not introduced in Italy until 1938. They are described in Michael A. Leeden, "The Evolution of Italian Fascist Antisemitism,"

Jewish Social Studies 37 (1975): 3–17; Ernst Nolte, *Three Faces of Fascism*, trans. Leila Vennewitz (New York: Holt, Rinehart and Winston, 1966), pp. 229–31. Mussolini had previously made various anti-Semitic remarks, but he had also declared himself to be opposed to anti-Semitism. See Ludwig, *Talks with Mussolini*, pp. 69–71.

66. Joly's *Dialogues* were published anonymously in Brussels in 1864. They are reprinted in translation in Herman Bernstein, *The Truth about "The Protocols of Zion"* (New York: Ktav, 1971), pp. 75–248.

67. Norman Cohn, *Warrant for Genocide* (New York: Harper and Row, 1967), p. 103.

68. Bernstein, *The Truth*, p. 84.

69. Ibid., pp. 83–84.

70. *The Jewish Peril: Protocols of the Learned Elders of Zion*, 3rd ed. (London: "The Britons," 1920), see especially pp. 1–3. Bernstein presents a side-by-side comparison of the paragraph from which this quote is taken in the *Dialogues* with the parallel passage in the *Protocols*. See *The Truth*, pp. 372–73. (Although Bernstein attributes the translation of the *Protocols* in his book to "The Britons," his text is not the same as that found their third edition.)

71. Bernstein, *The Truth*, p. 116. Emphasis in the original.

72. *The Jewish Peril*, p. 20. Also see Bernstein, *The Truth*, pp. 380–81.

73. *The Jewish Peril*, p. 5.

74. Ibid., p. 19.

75. A. C. Cuza, "The Science of Anti-Semitism," in Corneliu Zelea Codreanu, *For My Legionaries* (Madrid: Editura "Libertatea," 1976), pp. 37–43. The article originally appeared in *Apararea Nationala* 16, Nov. 15, 1922. Codreanu led the Rumanian Iron Guard; Cuza was his teacher and mentor until a split in 1924. Cuza briefly entered the government of Romania in 1937. See Joseph Rothschild, *East Central Europe between the Two World Wars*, vol. 9, in *A History of East Central Europe*, eds., Peter F. Sugar and Donald W. Treadgold (Seattle: University of Washington Press, 1974), pp. 308–11.

76. Cuza, "The Science of Anti-Semitism," pp. 37–38.

77. Examples of anti-Semitic riots attributed to the mob are given in Eleanore O. Sterling, "Anti-Jewish Riot in Germany in 1819," *Historia Judaica* 12 (1950): 105–42.

78. Cuza, "The Science," p. 43.

79. Ibid., p. 38.

80. Julius Langbehn, *Rembrandt als Erzieher*, 38th ed. 1891, p. 292. Cited in F. L. Carson, *The Rise of Fascism* (Berkeley: University of California Press, 1967), pp. 26–27.

81. Hitler, *Mein Kampf*, p. 276. Also see *The Speeches of Adolf Hitler*, vol. 2, p. 17.

82. Edmond Picard, *L'Aryano-Sémitisme* (Brussels: Paul Lacomblez, 1898), p. 76.

83. Karl Marx, *The Class Struggles in France 1848–1850* (New York: International Publishers, 1968), pp. 37, 46, 47, 49. *MECW* substitutes "wolves" for "Jews" in *The Class Struggles*, and "money-lender" for "Jew" in *The Eighteenth Brumaire*. Left-wing anti-Semitism in the nineteenth and early twentieth centuries is described by Edmund Silberner, "Two Studies on Modern Anti-Semitism," *Historia Judaica* 14 (1952): 93–118.

84. Hitler linked the Jews and the mob in Dietrich Eckart, *Der Bolschervismus von Moses bis Lenin: Zweigesprach zwischen Adolf Hitler und mir* (Munich: Hoheneicheu-Verlag, 1924), pp. 7–8. See also *The Speeches of Adolf Hitler*, vol. 1, p. 743.

CHAPTER 5

Fascist and Democratic Corporatism

Corporatism can be defined as an ideology that attempts to realize in practice the theoretical reconciliation of business and labor through its aim of organizing a state structure that allows their interests to be harmonized. Corporatism deliberately pursues a "third way" between liberal capitalism and socialism, typically through the development of tripartite political structures—composed of workers, their employers or managers, and the state—that are designed to limit or supersede industrial conflict. The history of this ideology in Europe since World War I presents a puzzle. On the one hand, it is associated with the rise of fascism and kindred movements and regimes between the wars, while on the other hand, it has influenced the development of institutions in West European democracies. This chapter explains the differences between these two types of corporatism by examining how the fascist form of corporatism has been structured around the distinction between the people and the mob, whereas democratic corporatism has been opposed to such a dichotomy. This examination extends the discussion of fascism found in the previous chapter and makes it possible to address the more general question of which forms of ideology are prone to distinguish between people and mob, and which are not.

Before entering into this analysis, however, it is necessary to justify my understanding of corporatism, which, while hardly unique, has been challenged by at least two well-known analyses. One is the Marxist contention that corporatism is the ideological expression of the petit bourgeoisie; the other is Philippe Schmitter's rejection of the idea that corporatism can be adequately defined as an ideology. It is to Schmitter's analysis that I turn first.

Schmitter defines corporatism as an empirical system rather than an ideology. It is

> a system of interest representation in which the constituent units are organized into a limited number of singular, compulsory, noncompetitive, hierarchically ordered and functionally differentiated categories, recognized or licensed (if not created) by the state and granted a deliberate representational monopoly within their respective categories in exchange for observing certain controls on their selection of leaders and articulation of demands and support.[1]

The reasons Schmitter gives for rejecting an ideological definition of corporatism, however, are both self-defeating. Schmitter lists forty-eight theorists who have advocated corporatism and concludes that they exhibit too much "normative variety" to allow for an ideological definition.[2] This argument, however, could apply equally to corporatist systems, and in fact Schmitter himself goes on to list eleven countries, such as Sweden, Chile, and Yugoslavia, that might be called corporatist. If this argument were valid, there would also be too much variety for corporatism to be defined empirically. It is invalid because it is possible to abstract a common definition out of a variety of different political doctrines in the same way that it is possible to abstract a common empirical definition from a variety of regime practices. Schmitter's second objection to an ideological definition is that advocates of corporatism have been *hypocritical*. But this objection, like the first, is self-defeating, as Schmitter describes fascist corporatism at least as a "facade"[3]; that is, its construction is hypocritical.[4]

This reopens the general question of the relative merits of defining corporatism as an ideology or a system. I would argue that an ideological definition is more helpful in tracing the forms taken by corporatism in Europe. Like socialism, corporatism has not emerged spontaneously as part of an established system but has been consciously constructed in theory and taken up by political organizations outside government before being incorporated into state practices. An institutional or systemic definition of corporatism, therefore, while not necessarily inaccurate, will be too narrow to deal with corporatism as an aspect of the ideology of political movements. It is true, as Chalmers points out, that postwar democratic politicians have tended to eschew the term "corporatism" because of its fascist connotations,[5] but this indicates merely that the concept has been given new labels, for example, the "social contract" of the 1974–79 British Labour government, or has been subsumed by broader terms such as "social democracy."

Schmitter's definition, however, is not only limited by its exclusion of ideology but also has particular problems associated with it. The definition rejects the idea that corporatism is concerned with structuring the relationship between labor and capital for the all-encompassing notion of the interest group. The only specific institution mentioned in the definition is the state. Corporatism appears to be a structure in which the actual composition of the "constituent units" is irrelevant. By excluding all mention of labor and capital, the definition incorporates the two pillars of behaviorism: the abstract system and the interest group. While this neatly locates the definition within the framework of assumptions underlying mainstream political science, it is also needlessly nebulous and, in fact, Schmitter himself rarely uses his own definition for the purpose of analyzing corporatist regimes, at least not in the abstract form in which he presents it. His actual, if unstated, definition is that corporatism is an institutional arrangement as he has ostensibly defined it, but one that has been constructed to serve bourgeois interests. Schmitter's implicit definition is considerably more fruitful than his explicit one. It allows him to link corporatist political practices to capitalist economic developments. However, this definition also tends to exaggerate the role of capitalist interests in structuring corporatism.

"STATE" AND "SOCIETAL" CORPORATISM

Before examining the relationship Schmitter identifies between bourgeois interests and corporatism, it is necessary to understand his typology and, in particular, his somewhat confusing concept of societal corporatism. Schmitter's famous distinction between "state" and "societal" forms of corporatism has served as a touchstone for many, if not most, of the subsequent academic studies of the subject. Schmitter associates state corporatism with the interwar and wartime regimes of fascist Italy, Nazi Germany, Austria under Dollfuss, and Vichy France, and societal corporatism with modern West European countries.[6] However, this apparent demarcation between corporatism in authoritarian or fascist regimes and corporatism in democratic regimes has several problems and cannot be accepted as it stands.

Schmitter describes how "state" corporatism is, as the term suggests, imposed and maintained by the state. By contrast, societal corporatism is depicted as developing piecemeal out of pluralism by interest groups whose recognition by the state is "imposed from below upon public officials."[7] The distinction seems clear: State corporatism is imposed on society, while societal corporatism develops through society and is imposed on the state. However, we then read that the development of societal corporatism

> can be traced primarily to the imperative necessity for a stable, bourgeois-dominant regime, due to processes of concentration of ownership, competition between national economies, expansion of the role of public policy and rationalization of decision-making within the state to associate or incorporate subordinate classes and status groups more closely within the political process.[8]

None of these developments refer to societal pressures from below; they occur at the highest levels of the bourgeoisie, in international rivalry, and in the apparatus of the capitalist state. Thus, it now appears that societal corporatism, like state corporatism, is imposed by the state. This is theoretically incompatible with Schmitter's description of societal corporatism growing out of pluralism. A "bourgeois-dominant regime" might operate in a formally pluralist system, but the essential feature of a truly pluralist system, the disbursement of power among divers competing groups, is irrelevant to the developments that are described as causing the transition to corporatism.

Of the two concepts of "societal" corporatism that Schmitter puts forward, the view that it emerges from society is the more attractive for analytical purposes, as it allows a clear distinction to be made with state corporatism. However, it is also more inaccurate. In his definition, Schmitter describes a trade-off for interest groups between recognition by the state on the one hand, and limitations on leadership selection and the demands that are made on the other. But who is to strike this bargain? According to Schmitter's first view of societal corporatism, the interest groups themselves are able to establish a de facto monopoly and use their position to demand incorporation into the policy-making process. But this assumes three things: first, that such incorporation is sought by these interest groups; second, that a corporatist system is more advantageous to these groups than one of pluralist conflict; and third, that these interest groups naturally develop monopolies within functionally defined spheres. All of these assumptions are highly questionable. A group that has been able to achieve a powerful position within a pluralist system may not be willing to abandon its *modus operandi* in return for state recognition. Its interests may be more effectively pursued through pluralist arrangements, the ideology of its members may make it resistant to any such incorporation, and it may define itself as a group in conflict with others rather than a functional unit. Such attitudes are exemplified by left-wing trade unions, by powerful business groups, and by their political allies; any account of the development of corporatism in postwar Europe must take these recalcitrant groups into account. Seen from this perspective, the development of corporatist institutions cannot be understood as evolving out of pluralist groups, as it depends on cutting out or marginalizing groups that may be powerful within a pluralist system. This can be done only at the level of the state, which therefore remains a key actor in the development of "societal" corporatism.

Corporatism and the Bourgeoisie

This brings us to Schmitter's second explanation of how societal corporatism, like state corporatism, emerges as the result of "basic imperatives" facing the capitalist state.[9] If state and societal corporatism are both seen as originating in the state, it becomes rather less obvious why one is associated with repressive and fascist regimes and the other with democratic ones, or indeed, how they can be distinguished at all. Schmitter's response to this problem—where he does not slip into the idea of societal corporatism as coming from below—is to associate the development of each type of corporatism with different forms of the capitalist state. State corporatism emerges from "delayed, dependent capitalist development and non-hegemonic class relations"; societal corporatism emerges from "advanced, monopoly or concentrated capitalist development and collaborative class relations."[10] This distinction, however, is untenable for three reasons. First, as has been explained above, it cannot simply be assumed that class collaboration will naturally develop under advanced capitalism. Class cooperation may be a consequence of societal corporatism, but it cannot be said to be a prerequisite to it. Second, the analysis of state corporatism relies on the questionable concept of state autonomy. Third, the assumptions that are made about relative levels of economic development are inapplicable to Europe.

Schmitter depicts the origins of state corporatism in Europe as being more or less equated with the rise of fascism. His argument can be traced, in part, to a misreading of *The Eighteenth Brumaire* that has been widely accepted since the publication of Nicos Poulantzas' description of "state autonomy" in *Political Power and Social Classes*. This misunderstanding of Marx's analysis juxtaposes the benefit of long hindsight into the nature of Louis Napoleon's regime with the attribution of scholarly foresight to Marx's quickly improvised and polemical pamphlet.[11] Hindsight suggests that the Second Empire was a regime that acted in the interests of the bourgeoisie and set the stage for continued bourgeois development, where, as Chapter 2 has shown, Marx argued that it would not act in bourgeois interests and would be superseded by a proletarian revolution. Because neither of Marx's predictions proved true, their role in structuring *The Eighteenth Brumaire* has been ignored. Instead, it has been incorrectly argued that the work explains the continuation of bourgeois dominance. Schmitter's misreading is typical of this type of argument.

It is certainly possible that a theory based on a misinterpretation of another work may nonetheless be valid. However, the problem with the misinterpretation of *The Eighteenth Brumaire* is the attempt to eat one's cake and have it, too. On the one hand, a state apparatus is posited that is independent of bourgeois interests; on the other hand, it is argued that such a state serves bourgeois interests. In the case of state corporatism, in interwar Europe, therefore, it is certainly plausible to use Marx's interpretation of Louis Napoleon's coup for the purpose of analogy and contend that the bourgeoisie supported the accession of a powerful fascist state to avoid socialism. What is not plausible is to argue that once the bourgeoisie had allowed the fascist state to become powerful, that it could nonetheless be relied on to safeguard long-term bourgeois interests. This, however, is the type of reasoning that Schmitter slips into.[12]

The distinction Schmitter makes between underdeveloped capitalism leading to state corporatism and advanced capitalism leading to societal corporatism does not fit particularly well with Europe. The description of state corporatism as the response to problems caused by delayed, dependent capitalism is clearly meant to refer to Latin America; it is far less appropriate in the case of Italy, Germany, Austria, and France in the interwar and wartime periods. Furthermore, Schmitter's idea that state corporatism crushes "incipient" forms of pluralism, while societal corporatism develops out of the "decay" of well-established "advanced" forms of pluralism, makes no sense in the European context. While it might be argued that pluralism was "nascent" in various European countries before the imposition of state corporatism caused its "demise,"[13] this makes it impossible to explain why these same countries, most notably West Germany and Austria, would become exemplars of societal corporatism in the postwar world.

It is possible to maintain a distinction between different forms of corporatism based on Schmitter's analysis by suggesting that there has been a differing potential for class compromise in interwar and postwar Europe. If the economy is weak, or in a depression like that of the 1930s, it is difficult for a corporatist regime to offer compliant trade unionists economic benefits that will enhance their reputation among the general union membership and marginalize their left-wing counterparts. Therefore, repression becomes a likely alternative. If the economy is strong or growing, however, as occurred throughout Western Europe after World War II, it is possible to avoid repression by rewarding trade unionists prepared to enter into corporate relations with management. If the state is seen as independent of the bourgeoisie (rather than being "autonomous"), the same relationship holds good with this class. Thus, we are left with a simple analysis, a continuum in which repressive forms of corporatism are inversely related and democratic forms of corporatism are directly related to national economic performance.

To revise the analysis of "state" and "societal" corporatism in this way, however, is only the first step in distinguishing between fascist and democratic corporatism. It is a model that greatly exaggerates the influence of economic circumstances by considering them as the sole determining factor. To better explain the difference between types of corporatism in Europe, therefore, it is necessary to return to the question of how they differ ideologically.

CORPORATISM AND THE PETIT BOURGEOISIE

Although the idea that corporatism is related solely to bourgeois interests has been rejected, another theory—ironically, one that also derives its inspiration from *The Eighteenth Brumaire*—needs to be considered. This theory is that corporatism in interwar Europe was the ideological expression of the petit bourgeoisie. (Advocates of this theory generally limit it to fascist forms of corporatism, as postwar democratic corporatism has been clearly supported by classes outside the petit bourgeoisie.)[14]

Toward the end of Chapter 3 is a quotation from a passage in which Marx associated the social democratic idea of class harmony with the interests of the petit bourgeoisie. In the same passage, Marx had written that despite the fact that social democracy envisioned

> the reformation of society . . . within the bounds of the petty bourgeoisie. . . . One must not form the narrow-minded notion that the petty bourgeoisie, on principle, wishes to enforce an egoistic class interest. Rather, it believes that the *special* conditions of its emancipation are the *general* conditions within which alone modern society can be saved and the class struggle avoided.[15]

This analysis has subsequently been extended to the interwar period, in which corporatist advocacy of a harmonious relationship between classes is seen as the political expression of the petit bourgeoisie. The theory has a certain intuitive plausibility; the location of the petit bourgeois class in the middle of the social scale, with the bourgeoisie on one side and the proletariat on the other, parallels corporatist ideologues' self-conscious rejection of the "natural" ideologies of these two classes, liberalism and socialism, for a "third way." However, such an analysis is rejected for two reasons.

The first reason is that the idea of class harmony is not limited to the petit bourgeoisie but extends to the working class, both in its scope of regulating the relationship between employer and employee and in its potential appeal. Marx himself admitted that visions of class harmony had some working-class support, but he believed that these supporters would be forced to adopt a more radical position by their material circumstances. Corporatist practice, however, in its fascist as well as its democratic form, has often been moderately economically successful.[16] It cannot, therefore, be assumed that the working-class supporters of corporatism will become radically disenchanted with their material position.

Second, the Marxist ideological agenda makes it tempting to make an *a priori* decision that popular anti-socialist movements and ideas are not supported by the working class. Attributing such support to the petit bourgeoisie provides a temptingly convenient alternative for ideological reasons, whether this explanation is justified or not. In this respect, the concept of petit bourgeois support for right-wing and fascist forms of corporatism resembles Marx's use of the lumpenproletariat to explain reactionary mass action in France. In fact, interwar Marxists, who were the first to link fascism to the petit bourgeoisie, were more or less equally divided in attributing the movement's mass base to the petit bourgeoisie, to the lumpenproletariat, or to both.[17] The evidence that these classes accounted for fascist support, however, is frequently no more than a simple assertion,[18] while a considerable amount of research into fascism in several European countries has found that a significant proportion of its popular support came from the working class.[19] In sum, corporatism cannot be reduced to the ideology of any one class.

THE COMMON BASES OF CORPORATISM

The ideology of corporatism has been rooted in criticism of both liberal-capitalist forms of government and the socialist opposition to them. Some of this criticism, such as that of the guild-socialists in England in the 1920s, has been both reactionary and utopian, and has had little political effect. The more influential strands of criticism have adopted first, a moral standard that has stressed social justice; second, a social and political theory of the role of a functionally differentiated society and a technocratic government; and third, an analysis of contemporary economic systems from the perspective of underconsumption theory.

The most famous advocate of social justice was Leo XIII, whose 1891 papal encyclical, *Rerum Novarum*, condemned rapacious employers for their exploitation of workers while upholding the right to own productive property. Unions were described as an acceptable method of defending workers' interests, provided they did not hold socialist objectives.[20] Belief in social justice had also long been manifested in popular demands for a "fair" wage, demands that reflected the view that a reasonable and socially just balance could be struck between the interest of employer and employee.

The theory of a functionally differentiated society and technocratic government was perhaps best known through the work and influence of Emile Durkheim.[21] While such theories did not have the same popular appeal as social justice, they were held by a significant number of intellectuals. In general terms, exponents of this perspective rejected the liberal theory of limited government for one that stressed rational planning, while socialism was criticized for fomenting class struggle by manipulating irrational passions.

Underconsumption theory gained currency during the Depression. Its most influential exponent was J. M. Keynes, whose main treatise on economics, *The General Theory of Employment, Interest, and Money*, came out in the mid-1930s.[22] Broadly speaking, underconsumption theorists argued that capitalism was prone to enter a cycle in which insufficient demand did not allow a nation to consume its potential productive capacity. Underuse of this capacity caused unemployment, which depressed demand further. The solution was to use government efforts to create demand in the economy.

Each of these three strands of thought has been reflected in the policies of democratic parties and governments in Europe, to some extent since World War I, but particularly since 1945. The post-World War II period saw widespread nationalization, which cut out private business interests and made it possible to pursue planned objectives. Conversely, unions were brought into government policy making, while at the same time, the attempt was made to reduce the influence of left-wing or communist politicians and union activists, both by political maneuvering and by formal proscriptions.[23] Within industry, employers or managers and unions were brought together in formal negotiating frameworks, while national policies reflected a commitment to full employment, sometimes in ways that required the cooperation of both management and unions through prices and incomes policies and limits on dividends.

The same three strands of thought were also reflected in fascist and authoritarian movements and regimes in the interwar period. They underlay state planning and intervention in industry, the establishment of vertical syndicates and industrial arbitration procedures, and the repression of independent, socialist unions. The combination of social justice, technocratic planning and underconsumption theory does not, therefore, provide the distinguishing feature of each type of corporatism but rather forms its common base. To distinguish between fascist and democratic forms of corporatism, it is necessary to identify further political beliefs and objectives, ones that impelled this common core of corporatist ideas in two different directions.

TWO TYPES OF CORPORATISM

One method of identifying the points of divergence between fascist and democratic forms of corporatism is to examine the dynamics of a transition in which critiques of the status quo shifted away from a democratic and toward a fascist perspective of political affairs. This transition occurred in several interwar corporatist movements, including: Oswald Mosley's British Union of Fascists; various political groups inspired by the economic writings of Major Clifford Hugh Douglas on "social credit"; and to provide a further point of comparison within the West, in the increasing anti-Semitism of Charles Coughlin's National Union for Social Justice in the United States of America. As the following extracts show, this shift took a similar form in each case.

In 1934, Mosley described a "crisis in the system" in Britain, one that he attributed to the rationalization of industry creating unemployment, and to underconsumption. This systemic crisis, Mosley argued, resulted in an economic cycle in which "booms of the present system will tend to get shorter and slighter in effect while depressions tend to get longer and more severe."[24] By 1939, however, Mosley's analysis of the economic cycle was very different. It was attributed not to abstract flaws in the system, but rather to the deliberate actions of financiers:

> By flux lives the financier and by flux dies the producer. The financier, in the inner ring, buys a the bottom and sells at the top. To him, therefore, it is essential that a bottom and top should exist, or, in other words, that flux should exist. The producer, however, before all else requires stability.
> . . . The ups and downs of the economic system, in what are called booms and depressions, are poison to industry but the life blood of finance.[25]

A similar shift is evident in the degeneration of Father Coughlin's popular Sunday broadcasts. Coughlin's generally systemic analyses of the Depression[26] became increasingly supplemented by the idea that the root of economic and social problems lay with a small financial class.[27] This class was distinguished from all others by being unproductive:

> A banker's brain . . . is identified with the non-creative things of this world. . . . Its functions are the functions of a sterile mule. The nail, the wheel, the wireless, the airplane, the benedictions of medicine, the artistry of surgery, the devisals of the engineer, the miracles of the chemist—all the steps in that patient progression from the squalor of the primeval swamp are the patient creations of the creators, the workmen of the world, not one of them of a banker.
> He has been the parasite that has lived by them and from them and in them.[28]

By the late 1930s, Coughlin—like Mosley—identified this banking class with the Jews.[29]

In his *General Theory*, Keynes concluded a historical survey of the underconsumption theorists who had preceded him by dismissing C. H. Douglas as "a private, perhaps, but not a major in the brave army of heretics" who had challenged economic orthodoxy.[30] Douglas' ideas, however, attracted a modest following of "green shirts" in Britain and had some international success.[31] In the years following World War I, Douglas had developed two main systemic analyses of the shortcomings of liberal capitalism. The first was called the "A + B theorem," a supposed proof that underconsumption was inevitable. Despite its flaws, this theorem became an article of faith among social credit followers. However, it was Douglas' second systemic critique of contemporary capitalism that formed the core of the development of much of social credit ideology.

Douglas' second critique followed the consequences of a temporary expansion of production by a manufacturer to fulfill an unusually large retail order. It was presumed that the manufacturer was breaking even, and that this required him to obtain a bank loan to fund the expansion. The bank, assuming that its depositors would leave enough money in their accounts to cover the sum of the loan, was able to supply the loan to the manufacturer by using these funds. The manufacturer then made the additional goods, sold them to the retailer, and repaid the loan, which was returned to the depositors' accounts. The result, Douglas argued, was that the purchasing power represented by the money used to supply the loan disappeared. This meant that the goods that were now on the market out-priced the amount of money that was needed to pay for them by the sum of the loan.

Douglas gave an example of this process at the 1929 World Engineering Congress in Tokyo. He described ten manufacturers, each with £100 in a bank, who conducted 90 percent of their business by check. One manufacturer then withdrew his £100 and an extra £100 loan to fund an unusually large wholesale order for goods. He made the goods, sold them, and three months later repaid £102 to the bank. (The £2 was the bank's profit.) The bank then restored the £100 to the accounts of the depositors who unwittingly supplied the loan. This created a situation in which the number of goods had increased without a corresponding increase in purchasing power.[32]

Four years after Douglas has presented his paper at Tokyo, the Irish writer, Eimar O'Duffy, published the political satire *Asses in Clover*, in which this analysis reappeared in a very different guise.[33] The world of O'Duffy's satire was controlled by the financier, Slawmey Cander, through the medium of the monopoly capitalist King Goshawk. Slawmey

Cander's financial activities were said to be the same in principle, if on a larger scale, as those of his ancestor, Ikey Cander. O'Duffy continued:

> This last, in the ancient times, having neither the will nor the ability to make anything worth making or do anything worth doing, . . . set up a bank. To this institution came sundry honest men, makers of bread, boots, bricks, books, and other good things, to place their hard-earned money in its care.

Then, following Douglas' figures exactly, O'Duffy described how a £100 loan was issued to Mr. Green, the bootmaker, and the money shortage that was created when the loan was recalled. O'Duffy described the consequences as follows:

> In order to fix a reasonable price for his boots, thus overloaded with costs, Mr. Green has to keep down the wages of his workers as low as possible; and in order to buy the necessaries of life, whose prices are all forced up by other bankers in the same fashion, the workers must try to get as high wages as possible. There is therefore continual friction between them, leading to strikes and lock-outs. When matters come to this pass, . . . both sides to the dispute have to borrow money from the Banker in order to carry on. The Banker—fairly splitting his black sides—creates it out of nothing as before.[34]

The starting point for the analyses of Mosley, Coughlin, and O'Duffy was an account of the failings of the liberal system, which identified abstract and impersonal forces as shaping economic circumstances in a way that was unrecognized and unplanned by the social groups that participated in the economy. This analysis was then transformed, not necessarily by abandoning it, but rather by adapting and supplementing it to stress the conspiratorial, *ad hominem* causes of economic depression. The problems of interwar capitalism were identified as stemming from the deliberate actions of specific social groups.

The transition from a systemic analysis to an analysis of a conspiracy was indicative of the tendency of fascist corporatists to give greater weight to voluntarist over systemic explanations of economic depression and industrial conflict. This shift also reflects a further transition on the question of who needed to be excluded from the corporatist state. Both fascist and democratic types of corporatism have advocated or practiced the exclusion of socialist unions and powerful business interests. However, where democratic corporatists have viewed the ideological (as opposed to systemic) sources of industrial conflict as emerging from within the relationship between employers and employees, fascist corporatists have argued that it originates beyond these groups.

Two of the main supposed culprits for the problems and conflicts that beset interwar Europe, according to Mosley, Coughlin, O'Duffy, and other advocates of fascist forms of corporatism, were the financier and his sidekick, the monopoly capitalist.[35] These classes were portrayed as a rich mob in a manner similar to Marx's definition of the finance aristocracy and big bourgeoisie. They were described as being unable or unwilling to participate in work and were consequently seen as a debased class.[36] Financiers, therefore, could be contrasted with the people, or workers and their employers, both of whom participated in useful work.[37] This distinction between the productive and the unproductive allowed the source of the antagonism that existed between productive groups to be located outside their economic relationship with each other, and attributed instead to the purposive conspiracy of the financial class. The further association between financiers and Jews drew on anti-Semitic conspiracy theories and depictions of Jews as "parasitic." This not only reinforced the concept of a deliberate, hidden source of economic depression and industrial conflict but also accentuated the separation between financiers and the people.

Although the rhetorical denunciation of financiers and monopoly capitalists is frequently found in fascist forms of corporatism, it has often been pointed out that once in power, fascists did not engage in a systematic attack on financiers and major capitalists, a fact that makes the significance of this distinction between fascist and democratic forms of corporatism somewhat more complex than it first seems. To explain this distinction, it should first be mentioned that the acceptance of the thesis that fascist forms of corporatism did not imperil financiers does not provide any evidence for the dichotomous conclusion that fascists and financiers formed an alliance. Even where it has been established that financiers contributed to political parties advocating fascist forms of corporatism, this can be interpreted as a defensive attempt at cooptation of already powerful movements, rather than a positive campaign to assist them to power.[38]

Once this has been established, the rhetorical difference between fascist and democratic forms of corporatism can be seen as part of a different dynamic between the operation of each type of ideology in and out of power. The fascist denunciation of financiers as being at the root of economic depression and industrial conflicts, while objectively false, was useful propaganda. It formed an integral part of the fascist appeal to the people as a nation of producers sharing common interests. Once in power, the fascists' ideological objectives shifted away from gaining political popularity toward the economic problems they had inherited. Their suppression of dissent and conflict directly within the industrial sphere, rather than through an attack on the sphere of finance, was a ruthless but nonetheless practical response to their new priorities.

Democratic corporatism has not shared this divergence between political rhetoric and actual policies. Its proposals for mitigating industrial conflict, like those of fascism, have been designed to appeal across class divides; they do not, however, make any significant use of hostile propaganda against unproductive groups outside industry. This orientation renders democratic corporatism less extreme. It has sought to moderate industrial conflict, where fascist corporatists have sought to end it.

The fascist denunciation of groups outside the people was not limited to a financial elite. As has been seen in the previous chapter, it included a denunciation of various mass groups as the mob. A further examination of this aspect of fascist ideology helps to explain why fascist forms of corporatism were anti-democratic.

One of the paradoxical features of the fascist form of corporatism was that at the same time as it identified the majority of the population as the people in the industrial sphere, it considered them a mob in the political sphere. This idea was somewhat more complex than the dichotomy between the financial mob and the people, because while the part played by the mob in a democracy referred to the majority of the population and not just a minority, the notion of the mob as separate from involvement in production was retained. To understand how this concept of the democratic mob was incorporated into fascist forms of corporatism, it is helpful to examine how it originated in the more conservative corporatist criticisms of mass participation in politics found in the nineteenth century.

In the discussion of crowd theory in Chapter 4, it was seen that a distinction could be drawn between the idea that each individual member of the mob was inherently capricious, violent, and so on, and the idea that these qualities appeared only in the aggregate. A similar distinction underlay the nineteenth-century corporatist critique of democracy, although in this case, it was not collective psychology that turned an aggregate into a mob but rather the way in which mass participation in democratic politics disengaged them from their group affiliations. Thus, Karl von Vogelsang said that modern liberalism had turned society into "a herd, a crowd and, if we look at the matter properly, a mob." He continued that the

> disintegration of the natural historic human organizations is what characterizes the mob. . . . To the extent that most modern peoples have dissolved their traditional organizations, instead of assuring their continued development, they have been transformed into mobs.[39]

One form of organization that prevented people from turning into a mob was found in the sphere of work. This emphasis on the importance of work organizations can be traced to Hegel, who argued that while the masses might be legitimately involved in political affairs through their participation in corporations (i.e., vertical trade associations), outside of these corporate units, they lost contact with the work that gave them a place in the state. The result of this loss of contact was that the majority of the population became disposed to make unreasoning demands on government or became the objects of political manipulation. As Hegel explained in *The Philosophy of Right*:

> The Many, as units—a congenial interpretation of "people", are . . . connected only as an aggregate, a formless mass whose commotion and activity could therefore only be elementary, irrational, barbarous, and frightful. When we hear speakers on the constitution expatiating about the "people"—this unorganized collection—we know from the start that we have nothing to expect but generalities and perverse declamations.[40]

Twentieth-century advocates of fascist forms of corporatism took up these criticisms of democracy and combined them with two further ideas. The first was to interpret elections and electioneering in terms of the crowd theory made popular by Le Bon. The second idea was their belief in a conspiracy that was naturally seen as extending to the parliamentary system. The resulting perspective saw democratic governments as the tools of finance, governments whose function lay not in their ability to handle complex administration but rather in their ability to conduct mass manipulation.[41] At the same time, advocates of fascist forms of corporatism were presented with a dilemma. The spread of universal adult male suffrage, which by the end of World War I had been adopted throughout most of Europe, meant that corporatism required some form of widespread appeal in order to be successful as a political movement within a parliamentary system. In other words, without a corporate structure in place, it was impossible for corporatism between the wars to appeal for popular political support without appealing to society as a mass.

The result of this dilemma was the development of a syncretic amalgam of two ideas. The first was that the voting masses were a mob whose members had forsaken their role as producers. The second idea was that the political actions of the masses expressed the virtues they exhibited in their work; that is, they were the people. These ideas were combined by the ideological attacks on financiers as the controllers of government. This simultaneously appealed to the "people" (defined as a group whose social characteristics placed them in a dichotomous opposition toward financiers) and explained why these same people, by participating in parliamentary elections, were the mob. It also provided the doctrinal justification for the paradoxical claim frequently made by interwar advocates of fascist forms of corporatism that the abolition of mass parliamentary democracy and its replacement with an occupational franchise restored government to the people.[42]

CONCLUSION

Schmitter's distinction between state and societal corporatism is of only limited use in distinguishing between fascist and democratic forms of corporatism in Europe. The analysis has several flaws, including its distinction between nascent and advanced pluralism, its contradictory understanding of societal corporatism, and its inability to explain corporatist movements. It does, however, suggest that different corporatist practices in Europe have reflected the depressed economic circumstances faced by fascists in the interwar period and the comparative prosperity of the West in the postwar period.

The idea that comparatively repressive or liberal forms of corporatism in Europe have reflected the economic context in which they operate needs to be tempered by an analysis of the ideological differences between fascist and democratic corporatism. The differences between these ideologies cannot be reduced to an analysis of the interests of the capitalist class or to the aspirations of the petit bourgeoisie. This is, first, because corporatism has gained cross-class support; and second, because the maintenance of the private sector in corporatist systems does not indicate that capitalist interests have been paramount. The maintenance of private enterprise is only one aspect of corporatist ideological objectives.

The generally shared tenets of corporatism have included social justice, rational planning, and an economic outlook that is indebted to underconsumption theory. Fascist and democratic forms of corporatism, however, have been shown to be distinct from each other in four significant ways. First, fascist corporatism has tended to stress voluntarist explanations of economic problems and conflicts, where democratic corporatism emphasizes systemic explanations. Second, fascists have supplemented the idea of the people united through their common participation in production with that of an unproductive elite group undermining the natural unity of the people, while democratic corporatism has generally located the source of conflict within industrial relations rather than outside them. Third, democratic corporatism exhibits a continuity between the presentation of its economic message outside power and its actions once in power, whereas fascist corporatist proposals to attack an unproductive elite are redirected toward repression within industry once they have assumed power. Fourth, fascist forms of corporatism have rejected electoral democracy for an occupational franchise.

Underlying these differences between fascist and democratic forms of corporatism is the comparative radicalism of fascist corporatism. While both forms of corporatism have criticized liberalism and socialism, the fascist critique has been more thoroughgoing. Considered in a simple and reductive form, liberalism has viewed unions as illegitimate, while socialism has viewed employers as illegitimate. By contrast, corporatism has viewed both unions and employers as legitimate. However, while democratic corporatism has also viewed the clash between unions and employers as legitimate, insofar as it forms an inevitable part of a relationship that encompasses both conflict and cooperation, fascist corporatism in Europe between the wars viewed unions and employers as being potentially fully cooperative, as both groups belonged to the people. Thus, fascist corporatism saw the source of any conflict as an illegitimate interference with this natural relationship.

Fascist corporatism, therefore, sought the complete harmony of a unified nation of producers. The degree of state control and repression undertaken by fascist forms of corporatism was, in part, a reflection of these utopian aims rather than a response to economic circumstances. By contrast, democratic corporatism has had a comparatively instrumentalist approach to work. It has not attempted to completely supersede group economic competition but rather recognized the legitimacy of sectional political action while attempting to minimize it.

The distinction between fascist and democratic forms of corporatism drawn in this chapter can be extended to suggest some broader conclusions about European ideologies. It raises the question of which ideological principles allow or encourage the dichotomy between the people and the mob, and which principles make an ideology unlikely to adopt such an analysis. The answer to this question depends, in part, on where an ideology lies on two continua. The first continuum has the aim of perfect societal harmony at one extreme and the contrary aim of a society in a state of constant internal conflict at the other. The second continuum lies between a societal analysis that assumes that social groups and their political objectives are defined by the moral outlook of their members at one extreme, and an analysis that assumes that the moral outlook of members of different social groups is either common to all of them or is irrelevant to their political activities at the other. Ideological principles that tend toward the first-mentioned extremes provide a structural basis with which to identify a people–mob dichotomy, while ideological principles that tend toward the second-mentioned extremes are incompatible with this dichotomy.

An ideology that aims for perfect harmony cuts across class divisions to define society as a united people, yet it invariably finds its supporters confronted with various degrees of societal conflict. One response to this gap between ideals and reality is to identify some of the protagonists in this conflict as being fundamentally illegitimate in their objectives or in their existence as a social unit. This response is epitomized by depictions of the mob. By contrast, an ideology that views group conflict as legitimate, as democratic corporatism does, or even as desirable, as pluralism does, has no underlying rationale to identify political opponents as an illegitimate outcast group. Similarly, the distinction between social categories on the basis of morality allows the identification of both the virtuous people and the wicked mob. By contrast, if morality is seen as uniform across groups or unrelated to their politics, it becomes irrelevant to social distinctions. However, the aims of pure harmony versus the acceptance of conflict clash with each other, and the perceived relevance or irrelevance of morality in group conflict clash with each other only when they are applied horizontally, that is, to the same thing. When these principles are applied to a range of phenomena, they may complement rather than contradict each other. The propensity to use the people–mob dichotomy, therefore, is not determined according to whether one or another principle is excluded from an ideology but rather by the extent to which each is applied.

The importance of the balance between endorsing harmony or conflict can be illustrated by considering parliamentarism. The acceptance of this doctrine by democratic corporatism rejects the fascist analysis of parliamentarians as the mob, rabble, herd, cynical manipulators of the mob, and so on. In this respect, the people–mob dichotomy is excluded. In another respect, however, the doctrine of parliamentarism itself could encourage the distinction between the people and the mob. Parliamentarism allows groups to conduct political conflict within mutually accepted limits. The common recognition of these limits establishes a higher level of harmonious agreement between competing groups. Harmony at this level is conceived as binding together society as a whole; that is, these limits are recognized and accepted by the great majority. To go beyond these limits in political conflict is to forsake the majority and to become an illegitimate minority. Thus, while the people may demonstrate, the mob riots.

The importance of the particular extent to which moral or structural divisions are used in political analysis can be illustrated by considering the ideological analysis of criminals. Michel Foucault has explained that in late eighteenth- and early nineteenth-century Europe, the concept of the offender, who commits a criminal act, was replaced by that of the delinquent, who adopts a criminal way of life.[43] The pervasiveness of this shift has meant that while ideologies might differ in their identification of criminal groups, or stress the structural conditions that lead to criminal behavior, there has been widespread recognition of an immoral criminal class. To some extent, therefore, exponents of almost all ideologies recognize the existence of a group akin to the mob. However, while some see criminals as irrelevant to structural political divisions, others might claim, as Cesare Lombroso did, that "the nucleus of almost all great rebellions is criminal. Moreover, criminals play such a part in parliamentary life that it would be impossible to eliminate them from it without great harm."[44]

An examination of the principles of an ideology, however, can only partially explain the use of the people–mob dichotomy, because one of the key characteristics of its use is that it is unprincipled. At various times, the distinction between the people and the mob has formed a pragmatic response to the reality of mass political power; allowed an explanatory flexibility that affirms ideological beliefs in the face of events that confound them; exploited subjective mass interests while defining these interests as fixed and objective; used the idea of the crowd as a middle state between "people" and "mob" to simultaneously repudiate and affirm the value of mass participation in politics; provided a method of justifying actions whose violence would otherwise appear reprehensible; and furnished a rhetorical device and practical technique for gaining mass support. In short, the ideological distinction being the people and the mob has been used in ways that are opportunistic, sophistic, hypocritical, and mendacious.

NOTES

1. Philippe C. Schmitter, "Still the Century of Corporatism?" *Review of Politics* 36 (1974): 93–94.

2. Ibid., pp. 87–89.

3. Philippe C. Schmitter, "Modes of Interest Intermediation and Models of Societal Change in Western Europe," in P. C. Schmitter and Gerhard Lembruch, eds., *Trends Toward Corporatist Intermediation* (Beverly Hills: Sage, 1979), pp. 72–73. Also see "Still the Century of Corporatism?" pp. 123–24.

4. If Schmitter had allowed himself to be influenced by Marx in his definition as well as in his actual analysis of corporatism, he might have concluded that instances of corporatist hypocrisy indicated precisely that it *was* an ideology. Schmitter, however, locates his definition firmly within behaviorism and thus appears to understand ideology as the manifestly stated, self-proclaimed tenets of a political doctrine.

5. Douglas A. Chalmers, "Corporatism and Comparative Politics," in *New Directions in Comparative Politics*, Howard J. Wiarda, ed. (Boulder, Colo.: Westview, 1985), p. 65.

6. Schmitter, "Still the Century of Corporatism?" p. 104.

7. Ibid.

8. Ibid., pp. 107–8.

9. Ibid., p. 107.

10. Ibid., p. 108.

11. Louis Napoleon staged his coup d'etat in December 1851, and Marx completed his pamphlet in March 1852. I describe the pamphlet as improvised because the coup and its immediate aftermath confounded the predictions Marx had made in *The Class Struggles in France*. Hal Draper makes the interesting suggestion that the work was improvised in a stronger sense of the word. Draper argues that the text shows how Marx's analysis of the coup changed as he was in the process of writing about it, so that the beginning and the conclusion of *The Eighteenth Brumaire* are somewhat at odds with each other. See Hal Draper, *Karl Marx's Theory of Revolution*, 2 vols. (New York: Monthly Review Press, 1977), vol. 1, p. 403.

12. Schmitter, "Still the Century of Corporatism?" p. 125. Poulantzas is cited in a footnote.

13. Ibid., pp. 106–8.

14. For example, see Bob Jessop, "Corporatism, Parliamentarism and Social Democracy," in *Trends Toward Corporatist Intermediation*, Philippe C. Schmitter and Gerhard Lehmbruch, eds. (Beverly Hills: Sage, 1979), pp. 205–6.

15. Karl Marx and Frederick Engels, *Karl Marx Frederick Engels Collected Works*. 50 vols. (New York: International Publishers, 1975), vol. 11, pp. 129–33.

16. The increasing strength of the German economy under the Third Reich is discussed in John D. Heyl, "Hitler's Economic Thought: A Reappraisal," *Central European History* 6 (1973): pp. 83–96; R. J. Overy, *The Nazi Economic Recovery 1932–1938* (London: Macmillan, 1982).

17. Explanations of all of these types are found in *Marxists in Face of Fascism*, David Beetham, ed. (Manchester, England: Manchester University Press, 1983). Further analyses that stress the role of the lumpenproletariat include Otto Bauer, "Fascism," in *Austro-Marxism*, Tom Bottomore and Patrick Goode, eds. (Oxford: Clarendon Press, 1978), and August Thalheimer, "On Fascism," trans. Judy Joseph, *Telos* 40 (Summer 1979): 109–22.

18. Richard F. Hamilton makes this criticism in the "Introduction" to his *Who Voted for Hitler?* (Princeton: Princeton University Press, 1982).

19. For analyses that stress the cross-class support for fascism in Germany, see Thomas Childers, *The Nazi Voter* (Chapel Hill: University of North Carolina Press, 1983), p. 265; Paul Madden, "Some Social Characteristics of Early Nazi Party Members, 1919–1923," *Central European History* 15 (1982): 48–49; Detlef Muhlberger, "Germany," in *The Social Basis of European Fascist Movements*, Detlef Muhlberger, ed. (London: Croom Helm, 1987), pp. 40–139. For Austria, see Gehard Botz, "The Changing Pattern of Social Support for Austrian National Socialism (1918–1945)," in Stein Vgelvik Larson et al., eds., *Who Were the Fascists?* (Bergen, Norway: Universitetsforlager, 1980), pp 202–225. For Switzerland, see Beat Glaus, "The National Front in Switzerland," in Larsen, *Who Were the Fascists?* pp. 467–78. For Hungary, see Istvan Deak, "Hungary," in *The European Right: A Historical Profile*, Hans Rogger and Eugen Weber, eds. (Berkeley: University of California Press, 1965), pp. 396–97. For Britain, see Stuart Rawnsley, "The Membership of the British Union of Fascists," in *British Fascism*, Kenneth Lunn and Richard C. Thurlow, eds. (London: Croom Helm, 1980), pp. 150–66. For Norway and Denmark, see Henning Poulson, "The Nordic States," in Muhlberger, *The Social Basis*, pp. 155–89. The general conclusion of these studies is that the middle class may have had a comparatively high rate of membership in the fascist parties. The working class can hardly be said to have been insignificant in its support, particularly when this is considered in absolute rather than proportionate terms. This conclusion is often supported

by an examination of the figures in empirical studies that stress middle-class support and de-emphasize that of the working class. For examples in the cases of Spain and Italy, see Stanley G. Payne, *Falange* (Stanford, Calif.: Stanford University Press, 1961), pp. 81–82; Marco Revelli, "Italy,' trans. Roger Griffin, in Muhlberger, *The Social Basis*, pp. 17–18.

20. Leo XIII, *"Rerum Novarum,"* in Anne Fremantle, *The Papal Encyclicals in their Historical Context* (New York: Mentor-Omega Books, 1963), pp. 166–95.

21. Emile Durkheim, *The Division of Labor in Society*, trans. George Simpson (New York: Macmillan, 1933).

22. John Maynard Keynes, *The General Theory of Employment Interest and Money* (New York: Harcourt, Brace and World, 1935).

23. See Victor Allen, *Trade Union Leadership* (Cambridge, Mass.: Harvard University Press, 1957), pp. 270–88; Scott Lash and John Urry, *The End of Organized Capitalism* (Madison, Wis.: University of Wisconsin Press, 1987), pp. 253–55; Keith Middlemas, *Politics in Industrial Society: The Experience of the British System since 1911* (London: Andre Deutsch, 1979), pp. 299–300, 406–7, 414n; Herbert Tint, *France since 1918* (New York: St. Martin's Press, 1980), pp 212–15.

24. Oswald Mosley, *The Greater Britain*, new ed. (London: British Union of Fascists, 1934), pp 67–69.

25. Oswald Mosley, *Tomorrow We Live*, 6th ed. (London: Greater Britain Publications, 1939), p. 34.

26. Charles E. Coughlin, *Eight Discourses on the Gold Standard* (Royal Oak, Mich.: Radio League of the Little Flower, 1933).

27. Charles E. Coughlin, *Eight Lectures on Labor, Capital and Justice* (Royal Oak, Mich.: Radio League of the Little Flower, 1934).

28. Charles E. Coughlin, *A Series of Lectures on Social Justice* (Royal Oak, Mich.: Radio League of the Little Flower, 1935), p. 66.

29. Charles E. Coughlin, *"Am I an Anti-Semite?"* (Royal Oak, Mich.: C. E. Coughlin, 1939).

30. Keynes, *General Theory*, p. 371.

31. The most comprehensive account of social credit parties in Britain, Canada, the United States, continental Europe, Australia, and New Zealand is found in Gorham Munson, *Aladdin's Lamp* (New York: Creative Age Press, 1945). Also see John L. Finlay, *Social Credit* (Montreal: McGill-Queens University Press, 1972). Crawford B. Macpherson, in *Democracy in Alberta* (Toronto: University of Toronto Press, 1953), presents a fascinating analysis of the development of social credit ideology and its changing orientation toward democracy. Although Macpherson's analysis is exceptionally well argued, I disagree with it for two reasons: first, Macpherson sees social credit as the political expression of the middle class; and second, he sees the development of social credit ideology in terms of "logic."

32. See Clifford Hugh Douglas, *The Monopoly of Credit* (London: Eyre and Spottiswoode, 1937), Appendix II, pp. 155–70.

33. Eimar O'Duffy, *Asses in Clover* (London: Putnam, 1933). The title alludes to the saying that "even asses wouldn't starve in a field of clover." The book is the third in a satiric trilogy, the other titles being *King Goshawk and the Birds*, and *The Spacious Adventures of the Man in the Street*.

34. O'Duffy, *Asses in Clover*, Book 3, Chapter 2, "The Machinations of Mr Slawmey Cander," p. 236.

35. For a further example, see the argument made in 1934 by the Belgian collaborator and Alpine hermit Hendrick de Man, *A Documentary Study of Hendrik de Man, Socialist Critic of Marxism*, Peter Dodge, ed. (Princeton: Princeton University Press, 1979), p. 304.

36. Oliveira Salazar, *Salazar Prime Minister of Portugal Says . . .* (Lisbon: SPN Books, n.d.), p. 50.

37. Ibid., pp 50–51.

38. For example, see the discussion of the money donated to Gyula Gombos in Hungary by Jewish bankers, in Joseph Rothchild, *East Central Europe between the Two World Wars*. Vol. 9 of *A History of East Central Europe*, Peter F. Sugar and Donald W. Treadgold, eds. (Seattle: University of Washington Press, 1974), p. 174.

39. Karl Von Vogelsang, *Die Sozialen Lehren des Freiherrn Karl von Vogelsang*, Wiard von Klopp, ed. (Vienna: Reinhold Verlag, 1938), pp. 167–68. Translated and quoted in Alfred Daimant, *Austrian Catholics and the First Republic* (Princeton: Princeton University Press, 1960), p. 57.

40. George W. F. Hegel, *Hegel's Philosophy of Right*, trans. T. M. Knox (London: Oxford University Press, 1967), paragraph 303.

41. For example, see John Gordon Hargrave, *Summer Time Ends* (London: Constable, 1935), pp. 820–59, especially pp. 847–50.

42. Benito Mussolini, *Fascism Doctrine and Institutions* (Rome: Araita, 1935), pp. 11–12; Salazar, *Salazar*, "Democracy," pp. 25–27.

43. Michel Foucault, *Discipline and Punish*, trans. Alan Sheridan (New York: Random House, 1979).

44. Cesare Lombroso, *Crime: Its Causes and Remedies*, trans. Henry P. Horton (Boston: Little Brown, 1911), p. 443.

Part II

DEMOCRACY

CHAPTER 6

Ideology and Democracy in the 1984–85 British Miners' Strike

In 1979, the "cosy" relationship between the Labour government and right-wing trade union leaders was abruptly terminated by the election of the Conservatives under Margaret Thatcher.[1] The National Union of Mineworkers (NUM), along with Britain's other unions, found itself faced with a government committed to imposing a liberal-capitalist regime on the country. One of the plain intentions of the new administration was to privatize Britain's nationalized industries, including coal mining. The first stage in this process was to make these industries run at a profit, regardless of the cost.

The confrontation between the NUM and the government began in February 1981. The previous year, the Conservatives had acquired, at enormous expense, the services of Ian MacGregor, a manager from the United States whose methods they much admired. Appointed to be chairman of British Steel, MacGregor attacked the industry and broke the strike, which was caused by the closures he had ordered. Flushed with success, the Conservatives supported a proposal by the National Coal Board (NCB), which managed the mines, to shut down as many as forty pits. The miners threatened to strike, and the Conservatives backed down.[2] Shortly after this confrontation, Joe Gormley, who had been the right-wing president of the NUM since 1971, announced his impending retirement. The left united to endorse Arthur Scargill as its candidate for the position. Scargill was elected president with 70.3 percent of the vote.[3]

Scargill's election to the presidency was the successful culmination of the left's long-term strategy to secure control of the national union. His powerful role in the NUM meant that it was no longer expedient for area officials to support right-wing positions at meetings of the 25-member National Executive Committee (NEC), and the right-wing "vote dwindled to five or six."[4] The government now faced an equally radical union. Each side was out to get the other. Scargill had a declared belief in conducting a "class war" against the state,[5] while the Conservatives, having fought and lost several battles with the NUM in the past, including the strike of 1974, which brought down the Heath government, were determined that it was a war that the government would win.[6]

THE POLITICAL GAP BETWEEN THE NUM LEADERSHIP AND MEMBERSHIP

Despite the election of a socialist president, there remained a considerable divergence between the policies that the new NUM leadership intended to follow and the views of the majority of union members. The left's popularity in the union had been achieved not because of its political views per se but rather because of its successful militancy in advancing wage claims and improving working conditions. As Scargill put it:

> They [miners] don't want to see anybody going onto a platform and yelling: 'I am a Marxist and I want to see dialectical materialism being brought in as the order of the day.' They couldn't bloody care less, but I'll tell you what they could care about: they could care about what's in their wage packet on a Friday, they could care about what their conditions are like. The very fact that we have been able to achieve all that we have won with a Marxist, progressive, left-wing leadership strengthens our movement.[7]

The official positions the left had gained as a result of this type of popularity were exploited to consolidate its control of the union by engaging in bureaucratic politics. Scargill, for example, moved the NUM headquarters from London to Sheffield, while firmly encouraging the London staff, recruited during Gormley's presidency, to stay in London.[8]

This is not to say that the left neglected the attempt to educate the work force by presenting arguments for socialism. Leftists had, however, deceived themselves over the extent of this method's effectiveness. The left perceived its contest to take control of the union away from the right not in terms of a struggle between two equally viable political doctrines but rather as a fundamentally asymmetric conflict between lies and truth. The right, it was argued, was unable to represent miners' interests effectively, because it lacked an appreciation of the class struggle inherent in capitalism. The right cooperated with management when the only appropriate method of dealing with it was to fight:

> The right-wing depended on apathy, on misinformation and on lack of information. The left-wing could only counter the right by providing information, by correcting false facts, and by clarifying the miners' position so that they knew what was happening to them.[9]

It was this perception of asymmetry that gave the left a false sense of complacency over the reception of its political message once it was in power. It underlay what Kahn has described as a mechanistic formula for directing the activities of the union.[10] This formula depended, first, on winning "leading positions"—and here the left has been successful. Second, these positions were to be used as a platform to explain left-wing political doctrine, mainly through speeches and newspapers. The third stage, the political radicalization of the work force, was then supposed to follow automatically. Socialist education, therefore, was seen as an unproblematic one-way transmission of doctrine and was carried out with a "surprising parsimony" of resources and effort.[11]

Symptomatic of this attitude was the left's heavy reliance on the speeches delivered by Scargill. The power of Scargill's oratory is well attested to. It was said that he could

> take a crowd and change them just like that [click]. He can go in there with the audience feeling hatred for him, and by the end of the meeting, they agreed with him. . . . Some would go down and say, 'I don't like him but I'll go and see what he has to say,' and by the end of the meeting they were all cheering.[12]

This type of reaction, however, suggests that the left misinterpreted the nature of the support demonstrated at such meetings. It was not the socialist message that gained supporters, but Scargill's grasp of techniques that would influence his audience. The support that Scargill generated—where he was not preaching to the converted—was the expression of a temporary crowd enthusiasm rather than a deepening socialist conviction. In sum, the left interpreted its institutional power as being indicative of a widespread socialist consciousness among miners, where in fact socialism remained a minority viewpoint.

Between 1981 and 1983, the left initiated three ballots over whether to hold a national strike. In each case, the NUM membership rejected striking. Despite Scargill's popularity, the majority of miners did not share the political perspective of the left. They were not prepared to strike in opposition to what, in light of subsequent events, were fairly minor cuts in the industry involving no compulsory redundancies.[13] Neither were they prepared to come out over wages while the Conservative government, wishing to avoid a strike until it had built up coal stocks, gave the NCB the latitude to offer comparatively high wage settlements.[14]

The first ballot, called for at a Special Delegate Conference in December 1981, while Gormley was still acting president, proposed a strike over a wage claim. It was rejected by 55 percent of voting union members in January 1982. The second strike ballot, in October 1982, combined the two issues of pit closures and wages in a single question. The left hoped that wage militancy could be tapped in support of a fight to resist pit closures. They were disappointed; 61 percent voted against strike action. In an almost identical result, 61 percent of voters rejected a third strike call, this time just over pit closures, in March 1983.[15]

It was not until after the third ballot that the government seriously began to threaten the nationalized coal industry. The change in tactics was signaled in September 1983, when the Conservatives appointed the manager of the steel strike, Ian "Butcher" MacGregor, as chairman of the NCB. The left saw the appointment, quite correctly, as part of a strategy to do to coal what had been done to the steel industry.[16] Scargill repeatedly warned of "a secret coal board hit list" of supposedly uneconomic pits, and predicted that the industry would lose between seventy and ninety pits and 70,000 to 100,000 jobs over the next four to five years.[17] At the end of the failed strike, in March 1985, 169 pits employed 170,000 miners. Four years later, there were 80 pits and about 70,000 miners left.[18]

THE STRIKE BEGINS

On March 1, 1984, the NCB announced that several pits were to be closed, including Cortonwood in Yorkshire. Local strikes were already taking place for various reasons at several nearby pits, and the left-wing Yorkshire-area NUM used the Cortonwood closure notice to coalesce these strikes into an area strike against pit closures in general. (The national union was formed by a confederation of area unions.) This in turn acted as a catalyst to the national strike, which is generally dated from March 12, 1984.[19]

The left's three previous attempts to initiate a strike had been based on Rule 43 in the NUM rulebook, which at that time required a national strike to be approved by 55 percent in a national ballot. (During the course of the strike, this figure was amended to a simple majority.)[20] A national ballot, however, was never held during the 1984-85 strike. Instead, the strike was spread under Rule 41, which authorized any striking area—in this case Yorkshire—to appeal to other areas for support. This rule required neither national ballots nor area ballots but allowed strikes to be spread through picketing.[21] Although several other areas conducted ballots on the strike, those areas that balloted and joined the strike generally did so despite the ballot result rather than because of it.[22] However, in Nottinghamshire, which had the second largest area union after Yorkshire, as well as in South Derbyshire, Leicestershire, the Midlands, and the North West, nearly all miners continued to work after area ballots in which the majority voted against striking. Overall, this meant that about 20 percent of NUM members were refusing to join the strike.[23] In Nottinghamshire and South Derbyshire, further ballots were held in which it was affirmed that these would not join the strike without a national ballot under Rule 43.

THE IDEOLOGICAL DEBATE DURING THE STRIKE

From the outset of the strike, the left-wing activists among the NUM had a detailed and coherent argument with which to challenge the liberal-capitalist ideology of the government and NCB. To some extent, this challenge was a technical one. It was argued that the NCB's cost-benefit analysis of pit profitability was deficient even on its own narrow economic grounds. At another level, however, the left was concerned to challenge the concept of defining a pit in terms of whether or not it was "uneconomic." To examine a pit in terms of abstract profit and loss was seen as ignoring the effect that closure would have on the community that centered on the pit. This, in turn, was seen as being indicative of the government's concern with profitability, which in general benefited

a narrow strata of shareholders and industrialists to the detriment of the
rest of the population. The Nottinghamshire miners' decision not to join
the strike, however, forced the left to split its ideological focus of attack.
The working miners threatened the success of the strike not only because
of the coal they were producing but also because they undermined the
NUM's appeal to other union members—notably railway, power, dock,
and steel workers—to respect picket lines or join the strike.[24] They also
called into question the popularity of the strike among miners to the
wider public.

The working Nottinghamshire miners did not fit into the left's critique
of government policy, and an accounting of them required an extension
of the ideological debate over the strike. The left did this by adapting
its ideological position to incorporate a dichotomous social distinction
between strikers and strikebreakers. Strikers were the people; strikebreakers were the mob. If "the people" refers to the majority, while "the mob"
is conceived as a distinct minority, it can be seen that in the absence of a
national ballot, there was a very uncertain basis for the left to make such a
dichotomy. It was precisely the lack of a ballot, however, that made such
a distinction an ideological imperative. The left's decision not to hold a
ballot had to be projected as irrelevant to the decision of Nottinghamshire
miners not to strike. This claim was externally important to the strikers
in their quest for support from other unions and from the general public.
It enabled the left to use the fact that the majority were on strike to
signify that the strikers, and not the working minority, represented the
people. The idea that the ballot was irrelevant was also important to the
strikers themselves, and in particular to those actively committed to the
strike, as it allowed them to retain the self-image that they belonged to
the majority. Finally, the ideological separation of the Nottinghamshire
miners from those on strike discouraged passive strikers in other areas
from returning to work. It was for all of these reasons that the strikers
and their supporters described the Nottinghamshire miners who broke
the strike as "scabs."

The "Scab" and the "Picket Mob"

The wider meaning of the term "scab" is rendered obscure by what
might appear to be an inarticulate hatred towards them: "They're a
different breed; they're just scabbing bastards all the way through. They're

just made up that way."[25] The problem in describing scabs was that in order to set them in opposition to the mass of miners, it was impossible to put forward the most obvious explanation for their motivation to break the strike: the absence of a ballot. This problem was solved by constructing a picture of Nottinghamshire scabs in which their calls for a ballot were symptomatic of their reasons for not joining the strike rather than their cause.[26] Thus, the Nottinghamshire miners were a socially distinct minority within the union; they were "a different breed." Their actions were not mistaken, but wicked; they were "bastards." Finally, they came to be seen as beyond redemption, as being pathologically opposed to the majority of mineworkers; they were "just made up that way." This was how the Nottinghamshire miners came to be depicted as the mob against the people.

In the first four months of the strike, Scargill believed that despite the enormous police operation to seal off Nottinghamshire pits from striking demonstrators, the working miners could be picketed into joining the strike.[27] During this period, the Nottinghamshire miners tended to be portrayed as thoughtless or stupid. They went to work like sheep, calling "Baaallot, baaallot" to the pickets at the gate.[28] Such depictions, hostile as they were, left open the possibility that the Nottinghamshire miners could be incorporated into the strike once they realized where their duty lay.[29] Increasingly, however, the miners were described as deliberately malicious in their pursuit of selfish, short-term interests, and their status as a wicked minority became established through epithets.[30] They were "maggots" or "scum."[31]

This split between the national NUM and the non-striking areas over the ballot was in fact the continuation of the struggle between the left and right wings of the union. Where strike activists saw the relations between labor and management as essentially combative, the Nottinghamshire leaders favored a comparatively cooperative relationship. They were corporatists rather than socialists, insofar as they recognized that management had a legitimate function in running the industry.[32] However, the compelling reasons that the strikers had to depict the Nottinghamshire miners in extreme terms as a deviant minority meant that, just as they could not explain the area's defection from the strike in terms of the ballot, so they could not characterize the split between the national leadership and the leaders of the strikebreakers in terms of an argument between socialist and corporatist doctrine. While such a characterization might have allowed a substantive debate to take place, this would have undermined the picture of the Nottinghamshire miners as scabs.

It is ironic, therefore, that throughout the strike, the NUM leaders charged the government, NCB, and media with obscuring the "real issues" involved in the dispute—that is, the debate over pit closures— by constantly vilifying those on strike as a mob. In fact, the strike activists themselves created the physical and ideological conditions that made the description of them as a mob by their opponents an effective propaganda tool. First, in the absence of a ballot, the left's policy toward Nottinghamshire relied on mass picketing and the physical confrontation of working miners with strikers. Second, the dichotomy between strikers and scabs put forward by the left changed the structure of the debate over the issues being contested in the strike. The polarized positions of the NUM and government no longer defined the terms of this debate but became just one of its dimensions, alongside the polarization between strikers and strikebreakers as people and mob. Thus, when opponents of the strike extolled the working miners and described the strikers as lawless thugs, they were operating within the ideological structure created by the left. They did not shift the ground on which the ideological debate was being conducted but simply inverted the depictions of the sides involved. The working miners were the people; the strikers were the mob.

A comparison of two later accounts of the same event illustrates the mirror image that each side held of the other. During a confrontation between strikers and working miners at the Nottinghamshire area head-quarters in Mansfield, the financial secretary of the area, Roy Lynk, made a speech. Unlike the Nottinghamshire General Secretary Henry Richardson and President Ray Chadburn, Lynk supported the working miners. Strike sympathizers Jonathan and Ruth Winterton wrote of the incident:

> The right-wing backlash in the Notts area became evident of 1 May 1984 when about 7,000 working Notts miners demanding the resignation of Chadburn and Richardson clashed with half as many strikers. . . . Lynk, formally unauthorized to speak, snatched the microphone and encouraged the mob haranguing Richardson and Scargill.[33]

By contrast, in his book on the strike, *The Enemies Within*, Ian MacGregor wrote that Lynk "managed to get to the microphone and tell the working majority in the crowd to stick to their guns and he would support them, before he was dragged off under a hail of missiles and spit."[34]

MacGregor's perception of "the mob,"[35] otherwise described as the "howling mob," "rabble," "the rag tag mob of the militant left,"[36] while rooted in the violence of the picket line, blended into a mixture of popular myth and bourgeois nightmare in which dark fears surfaced with the sudden appearance of "a sinister mob of almost-uniformed anarchists— led by a woman."[37] His description of the short speech of Roy Lynk, however, with its contrast between "the vast majority who wished to work"[38] and the ugly violence of the striking minority, is typical of the way in which various critics of the strike, including members of Parliament, working miners, officials of other unions, and the press, identified pickets with "the mob." The common starting point for these criticisms was the condemnation of picket line violence. The strike activists who engaged in such violence were then invariably identified as a minority. At this point, critics of the strike diverged by defining the minority status of violent pickets in three different ways. Occasionally all strikers were defined as a minority mob. More often, however, pickets were separated from the majority of strikers who engaged neither in violent picketing nor in any strike activities. A third way of defining pickets as the minority was by making prejudicial references to the infiltration of the picket line by outsiders.[39]

The collective threat posed to the strike by scabs was that they engaged in productive work. Given this, it is not surprising that the characteristics of being useless and idle, which are commonly attributed to the mob, were not used to depict the Nottinghamshire miners during the strike. However, these characteristics were sometimes evoked in hostile depictions of strike supporters. Labour Party leader Neil Kinnock, for example, described left-wing groups that had attached themselves to the strike's cause as "parasites,"[40] while a Union of Democratic Mineworkers (UDM) officer from Derbyshire later described that "rent-a-mob was there [at the picket line]: Loughborough students, Militant, WRP, and a notorious South Derbyshire family who'd never done a days work in their life."[41]

Less frequently, NUM pickets were also described as workshy: "They don't want work, they're just tap room men."[42] But this contrasted with the popular image of how miners in general displayed the qualities of the people writ large. Miners were seen as hard-working, productive, and heroic, as "men who wrest a living from the earth."[43] Defining pickets as a distinct minority within the NUM therefore performed a crucial ideological function in promoting opposition to the strike. Rather than attempting to redefine miners in a negative way, opponents of the strike were able to frame their position in a way that affirmed that not only the working miners but also most of those on strike were the *people*.

The absence of a ballot was pivotal to the ideological separation of pickets from the majority of strikers, as it made it difficult for the pickets to claim an explicit majority mandate for their actions. The NUM leadership of the strike claimed that such a mandate was demonstrated by the fact that 80 percent of miners had joined the strike. But without a ballot, it could be countered that this majority did not justify picketing, as it had only been gained through picketing. The overall effect of the decision not to ballot was therefore doubly unfortunate for the left leadership of the strike. Not only had it forced the leftists to add a people–mob dichotomy to the ideological debate over pit closures, but it had simultaneously undermined their claim to be the people and bolstered the opposite image of pickets as the mob.

The strategic advantage that the absence of a ballot gave to opponents of the strike was appreciated by MacGregor, who concluded his explanation of ostensible NCB efforts to organize one with the comment that "there was one other reason for suggesting we should ballot the men ourselves: it helped Arthur Scargill make up his mind not to."[44]

Why then did the left decide not to ballot? Did it involve something more than the obvious explanation that after three previous national strike calls had been rejected, a further ballot was predicted to fail? To answer this question, it is necessary to reconstruct the theoretical views and reasoning process that underlay the ideological positions taken by the left of the NUM during the strike.

"Democracy" and the "Rank and File"

The NUM leadership employed two main slogans to defend spreading the strike under Rule 41 (picketing) rather than Rule 43 (balloting). These were first, that "you don't vote another man out of a job"; and second, "the cardinal rule of trade unionism is that workers do not cross picket lines." The principle embodied in the first slogan implicitly recognized that those who were willing to strike may have been in a minority. (Quite apart from the problem of getting miners to believe that there was a huge pit closure program planned in the face of bland NCB denials, even the left doubted Scargill's worst-case prediction that it would reduce the work force by over 50 percent.). The principle embodied in the second slogan was designed to turn this possible minority into a unanimous majority, for taken to its extreme, it allowed for the unlimited expansion of the number of workers on strike. The reliance on picketing rather than balloting to spread the strike was not, of course, dependent solely on the principled refusal of trade unionists to cross picket lines. If this had been the case, a secret ballot would merely have affirmed a similar principle of solidarity. In fact, spreading the strike under Rule 41 was effective because it combined the appeal of siding with the majority with coercion.

The methods that were used to spread the strike were based on the "flying picket" tactics that the left had developed in Yorkshire during an unofficial strike in 1969.[45] During this dispute, hundreds, sometimes thousands, of striking pickets would arrive unexpectedly at an industrial site not involved in the controversy and prevent the workers from entering. The strike leaders would then attempt to persuade the union officials at the site to endorse the strike. Finally, leaving a token presence at the gates of the industry that had been closed, the pickets would fly on to somewhere else. This tactic worked fairly well, but to understand its success it is necessary to examine an apparent paradox in the process. If the sudden appearance of hundreds of pickets at an industry was designed to be coercive, to make it physically impossible for workers to get to work, why did these workers not return to work after the bulk of the pickets had left? Sometimes, it is true, the workers did go back, but even where pickets had failed to reach an agreement with local union officials, this was not always the case. Workers stayed at home because the flying pickets combined an implicit coercive physical threat to return, with a more intangible but nonetheless potent appeal to join the strike.

Some members of the left explained this appeal as being directed at working-class unity: Picketing raised workers' consciousness of their class position, and those who were picketed out were persuaded by the idea of joining in a class struggle. To transmit such ideas, however, requires reasoned argument, a form of dialogue that tends to vary in inverse proportion to the numbers of pickets at a gate.[46] It can be argued, therefore, that working-class unity is a slightly misleading description of the appeal to strike, and that the fundamental impression conveyed by the physical presence of large numbers of pickets was rather an appeal to the democratic impulse to side with the people, to identify oneself with the majority. Given this argument, it can be seen that a flying picket of successive single industrial sites was more effective than disbursing small numbers of pickets over many sites, not only because large-scale picketing was coercive but also because it allowed an activist minority to take on the appearance of the majority.

In 1969, the unofficial strike was prematurely ended by a ballot vote that resoundingly rejected making it official.[47] The left were determined that this type of rebuff would not happen in 1984. This was made evident at an NEC meeting on 12 April 1984, when the right-wing president of the Leicester area, Jack Jones, proposed that the NEC call a national ballot. In the weeks leading up to the meeting, a narrow majority of NEC members had been given area mandates to vote in favor of a ballot, even though most of them, as individuals, supported the decision not to hold one. Faced with this problem, Chairman Scargill simply declared that Jones' motion was out of order. Jones challenged Scargill's decision and lost by sixteen votes to eight; the opponents of the ballot reasoned that while they may have been mandated to vote for a strike, they had not been mandated to overrule the chair on a point of procedure.[48]

The avoidance of a ballot reflected the widespread agreement by strikers and their supporters that holding one could only favor their opponents. Thus, it was claimed that even had the ballot result been successful, it would have made no difference to the Nottinghamshire miners' decision to work. However, while the *realpolitik* of the left helped them to defeat the right's attempt to hold a ballot, they saw the strike not as an extension of the bureaucratic political maneuvering that had aided their rise within the union but rather as the attempt to move beyond politics conducted at this level. Despite the lack of a ballot, the strike was seen as a step toward a more democratic struggle for socialism, one involving widespread participation.

This conclusion might appear odd, given the way in which the left exploited its institutional positions at all levels within the union during the strike. At Creswell in Nottinghamshire, for example, the left-wing branch officials attempted to engineer a vote in favor of strike action by calling for a mass meeting to vote on the strike by a show of hands at a time that most of the work force was at the main morning shift and the rest were intimidated by the pickets who had arrived in the village.[49] But tactics such as these were not perceived as subverting democracy by the leadership. The strike, it was argued, was democratic because of the way in which it had been spread by the "rank and file," that is, by active strike supporters outside the union hierarchy. Therefore, the bureaucratic methods used to avoid a ballot were seen as defending what was democratic about the strike from becoming contingent on an ideological debate over the strike conducted at a national level. Such a debate, it was argued, would allow the anti-strike forces a considerable undemocratic advantage, particularly because these forces were aided by a sympathetic national media.

To explain why the left held these views, it is helpful to return to the strikes of the 1970s. In 1972 and 1974, two national strikes had occurred under Joe Gormley, a right-wing president with a right-wing majority on the NEC. On both occasions, Gormley and the NEC had recommended strike action to the membership.[50] The left, however, never accepted this public posture as genuine. Gormley and the NEC, it was said, did not want the strikes, which were forced on them: "They could not stop the pressures from below."[51] The strike ballots that were called by the NEC were seen as being subsequent to this pressure. Therefore, in the eyes of the left, it was not the ballots per se that legitimized the strikes, but the "rank and file" who had forced the right to hold these ballots in the first place. The left saw the 1984 strike as originating and spreading through the same type of pressure, although in this case the pressure was simply for a strike and not for a ballot.

It has been argued that the left had a mechanistic concept of spreading socialism among union members, one that assumed that mass acceptance of socialist ideas would be virtually automatic once they had been authoritatively presented. The failure of the strike ballots in the early 1980s, however, forced the left to revise this position, while retaining the implicit underlying concept of miners' political views as being malleable. The left's revised viewpoint gave greater weight to the effect of hostile propaganda originating outside the union, with the right-wing media singled out as having a particular influence on miners' political outlooks.[52] This provided a further reason not to hold a ballot, as it led to the conclusion that union ballots were largely decided by undemocratic and external institutions and were not therefore truly democratic. Given this conclusion, the "solidarity" achieved by the rank-and-file in picketing 80 percent of the work force out on strike was seen as being democratic because of the level at which mass participation in the strike had been achieved. Democracy was defined as political action that came from the bottom up rather from the top down. Balloting was seen as a form of political action that would be determined at the top end of an elite–mass political spectrum, one in which the national leaders of the NUM would have to compete against the influence of hostile outside interests—the government, NCB, and press. Picketing, by contrast, was seen as epitomizing political action that came from the bottom.

Implicit in this understanding of democracy was the assumption that political action that came from the bottom up would be supportive of socialist objectives. The rank-and-file, therefore, while it might have been in a minority in terms of numbers, was seen as representing the interests of the majority. From this premise it is understandable, if not logical, that some union officials and strike activists deduced that the rank-and-file represented the will of the majority. This in turn allowed a further step: the conclusion that the rank-and-file was the majority.

Two factors encouraged this theoretical conclusion. The first was that the rank-and-file, by definition, referred to those outside the union hierarchy. Therefore, if elite politics was equated with those who held formal positions in the union, the activism of the rank-and-file did not separate them from other miners. The fact that the rank-and-file had chosen to become active in the strike did not mean that it became a self-defining minority but rather appeared to remain indistinguishable from the majority. The second factor that encouraged such a conclusion was the affinity it had with the left's position in the ideological debate over identification of the people and the mob. Without a ballot, the rank-and-file's claim to represent the decision of the majority was weakened. The idea that the rank-and-file was typical of striking miners in general, therefore, provided an alternative method of identifying strike activists with the people.

MAINTAINING THE STRIKE IN LOCAL COMMUNITIES

Although the equation of the rank-and-file with the people was a necessary component of the national ideological debate, at a local level, the same equation could result in confusion over the methods that were used to ensure that the strike remained solid. This was made clear by the gap between rhetoric and reality concerning the community. Some commentators on the strike have argued that underlying solidarity for the strike at each pit was a sense of community rather than working-class consciousness.[53] This point can be extended to suggest that at an ideological level, the concept of the community was the local equivalent of the national concept of the striking miners as the people. As an analytic concept, however, the idea of the community needs to be modified, as around each pit there existed not one community but two. One community was formed by active strikers, while the other contained passive ones. This division has been suggested in a book written by "the people of Thurcroft" (by which is meant, "the activists of Thurcroft"),[54] in which Peter Gibbon and David Steyne explain that "between the inner community of activists and the wider communities of miners and their families, there were strongly contrasting experiences of the strike."[55] They explain that the descriptions by activists of how they made friends with each other and enjoyed themselves contrasted with "the dourer and more private and restricted experience of the majority" of the villagers.[56]

Given these two communities, it can be argued that for activists to enforce the strike at a local level, they needed to first maintain their own enthusiasm for it, and then coordinate their efforts to use whatever means were necessary to prevent the non-activist majority from returning to work. The identification of the activists with the people meant that these two objectives became confused. Resources that were used to maintain activists' own commitment to the strike were seen as supporting the people as a whole. Thus, strike funds were distributed on the picket line,[57] and food kitchens were monopolized by the families of activists.[58] Added to this was an ethos held by some activists that it was legitimate to ensure that those involved in maintaining the strike (i.e., themselves) deserved some reward for their efforts. This further skewed the distribution of general resources, including food donations and money raised in street collections, toward members of the activist community.[59] The result was that the central method of maintaining the strike among the majority of the work force was not through the distribution of resources or involvement in communal activities but was rather through coercion.

In August, a few miners from areas solidly on strike began to return to work. The explanation for their return offered by activists emphasized their status as a distinct minority by pointing out that many of these strikebreakers came from outside the community.[60] While it may have been true that the first strikebreakers tended to live outside pit villages,[61] the significance of this location might be better described not so much in terms of being outside the local community but rather as being comparatively isolated from the pressure to support the strike imposed on this community by activists.

The methods that were used to inhibit local strikebreaking tended to differ from those that had been used against the Nottinghamshire miners. The violence of the picket line at working pits and other industries, while in part ideologically motivated, planned, and organized, also escalated as a dynamic response to violence by the police, provocations by working miners, and by crowd excitement. Violence and other forms of coercion against individual strikebreakers, however, was carried out deliberately and systematically. It included vandalizing property, ostracism, insults, assaults, and attacks on family members.

The ideology that justified this type of violence can be illustrated by an activist's account of what happened when he and other members of "the scab watch team" confronted suspected strikebreakers on their doorsteps:

> You soon knew if you were right . . . scabs all stuttered and a definite sign was shit seeping from their trouser legs. (Some wised up and took to wearing bike clips, but the smell was still there.) The excuses used by them were nearly always the same:
>
> > No money
> > No help from the union
> > Scargill's strike.[62]

In earlier chapters, it has been seen that excretory metaphors have frequently been applied to the mob to reinforce its abstract categorization as a repellent social group outside the body of society. In this depiction of the scab, this symbolic quality is personalized and described as being literally manifested on confrontation with the community. The way in which the strikebreakers' three typical excuses are described as being refuted establish that it is the community that condemns them and not simply the local activists. Thus, (1) the skewed distribution of resources toward strike activists is ignored, and it is said that no one has any money; (2) the mutual support activists provided to each other is universalized, and it is said that the union has given help; (3) to attribute the strike to Scargill is said to be a media lie—it is left to be inferred that the strike came from below.[63]

Once it has been established that strikebreakers are outside the community, the final step is to define the retribution of the community as a defensive measure against the "violence" that had been done to it: "The community was the strength of the strike, a person standing among his workmates and neighbours was part of his character and life, to abandon the community and cross the line was to take a violent turn against the community."[64]

In sum, while the community of activists maintained its commitment to the strike through the activists' extensive use of various support mechanisms, they maintained the strike among the wider community through the threat of violence, while they defined themselves as being at one with that community. This ideology went unchallenged in the pit villages until the number of miners forced back to work by poverty was sufficient for them to be able to form a viable community of their own, one through which they could dispute the activists' definition of themselves as the people.

Before this stage was reached at a pit, strikebreaking typically increased gradually and arithmetically. After this stage was reached, strikebreaking tended to expand geometrically.

REDEFINING THE MINORITY AFTER THE STRIKE

The first strikebreakers had been defined as irrevocably separated from their community by strike activists, and in those pits where only a few returned to work, this stance was maintained after the strike.[65] However, by the time the strike ended in defeat in March 1985, just over half of the NUM was already back at work.[66] In pits where there had been a widespread return to work, a few activists remained adamant in their rejection of scabs. As one explained five years after the strike had ended: "Majority what work here I don't talk to. Anyway in my job I'm on my own. [This was not a coincidence.] . . . I haven't spoken to my best man since December 4th 1984 when he went back."[67]

Other activists attempted to redefine an outcast minority among the strikebreakers, for example by identifying " 'superscabs' who returned before Christmas, and certain particularly obnoxious individuals who returned afterwards."[68] This approach, however, was rendered less effective by the strikebreakers themselves, who singled out activists as having formed a narrow clique that had, comparatively speaking, benefited from the strike:

> I heard a lot of stories, after I went back, of union men feathering their own nest, . . . getting a set of new tires and taxation for a car used to transport pickets, . . . fiddling money from collection boxes, . . . distributing food parcels to the friends of union men.[69]

One Yorkshire miner who stayed out the length of the strike said that "there were so many went back that the whole thing about being a scab were reversed. We were scabs. . . . We were the traitors, the outsiders."[70]

In Nottinghamshire, the same reversal took place: "The miners turned the tables on the pickets; as they went into work they shouted at them: 'Wait until the strike is over and we'll bloody wallop you.' And they did too. And it served them right."[71] In the following months, those strikebreakers who had always been in a small minority at a pit were often either forced out of mining or transferred to another area after "nightly pressure from the community."[72] However, where the strike had initially been fully supported but where large-scale strikebreaking had later occurred, a different process took place. Despite the bitter rhetoric of the dispute, miners in these pits generally seem to have made a conscious decision to forget who were the people and who were the mob: "I was still fired up after the strike and caused a furor. I wrote on my helmet, 'I supported my union, did you?' . . . After a few weeks I changed my helmet."[73]

The Formation of the Union of Democratic Mineworkers

After the strike ended, the left faced a dilemma in Nottinghamshire. They wished the area to remain in the national union but also wanted to expel the officials who had led the opposition to the strike. Well aware of this threat, the Nottinghamshire officials had already begun a legal process to separate the area from the national union. For the national NUM to prevent this, they could no longer refer to Nottinghamshire miners in general as scabs without alienating them from the union. If the miners were to be dissuaded from voting themselves out of the union, the leaders of the strikebreakers had to be identified as a wicked minority who were separate from the Nottinghamshire miners as a body.[74]

There remained some loyalty to the national union among working miners, as well as an appreciation of the benefits of being represented by a single national federation in negotiations with the NCB, and the national NUM attempted to capitalize on these advantages in its propaganda. There were, however, two problems with the union's campaign. The first was that the tactical need to redefine the minority in Nottinghamshire was not fully appreciated at lower levels of the union. Local officials and activists continued to publicly condemn strikebreakers in extremely derogatory terms, and a few went on expeditions into the area to deface property. This exacerbated the second problem, which was that the Nottinghamshire officials, in their campaign to get support for a new union, stressed not that their own careers were at stake, but rather the way in which the national union had depicted all who had worked during the strike as scabs. The propaganda statements made by the NUM during the strike were turned against them. Through leaflets and the area newspaper, the Nottinghamshire miners were continually reminded of comments such as those directed at strikebreakers by Author Scargill: "You will become lepers, . . . outcasts. . . . You will be stained to the end of time."[75] In October 1985, three areas—Nottinghamshire, South Derbyshire, and the Durham Mechanics—voted to amalgamate to form the Union of Democratic Mineworkers. The NUM had not only lost the strike but had failed to prevent the splitting of the union.

THE FAILURE OF THE STRIKE

The forces that were arrayed against the NUM during the strike were considerable. The Conservative government was both better prepared and more ruthless than it had been in the strikes of the 1970s. Saturation policing, mass arrests, the denial of welfare benefits, the building up of coal stocks from abroad, and revised trade union legislation all made a successful strike more difficult. However, the NUM lost the strike not simply because of these external factors but also because of the dynamics of the political strategy followed by the left. This strategy was seen as following three loosely sequential aims: first, achieving control within the union; second, altering the political orientation of the majority of union members; and third, engaging in the mass struggle for socialism through adversarial union activity. While the left had been successful in its first aim of securing leading positions in the union, once in power, its political views remained to the left of most of the membership's. This meant that the left's effort to shift to its third objective was somewhat contradictory, as in order to escape the influence of the capitalist media, it did not hold a democratic ballot, while in order to get the majority of the work force on strike, it used the coercion of an activist minority.

The left's misinterpretation of the nature of its support was the result of the clash between idealism and *realpolitik*. Thus, the left explained its support before and during the strike by using a classic socialist analysis of working-class consciousness, although this support had in fact been achieved and maintained through other means. The militancy that the miners had shown over wages and conditions before the strike was seen as indicative of an incipient socialist consciousness rather than an end in itself. During the strike, however, socialist activists gathered at a meeting or picket line were seen as representative of general working-class sentiment. Oligarchic forms of political organization were defined as popular grass-roots initiatives; crowd excitement was seen as class commitment; and behavior resulting from coercion was seen as action springing from conviction. Such misinterpretations were simultaneously useful as external political propaganda and the maintenance of political beliefs, and problematic insofar as they formed the theoretical basis for the actions of those involved in the strike.

The dichotomous depiction of striking miners as the people and working miners as the mob expressed this dilemma. The dichotomy allowed strike activists to deny that their decision not to ballot was relevant to the decision of the Nottinghamshire miners not to strike, a denial that was necessary both to the self-identification of activists with the majority and to the projection of the claim that the strike was supported by the most miners. At the same time, the dichotomy was problematic for at least two reasons. The first problem was that the activists' view of themselves as at one with strikers in general encouraged them to benefit disproportionately from the resources that enabled the miners to stay out on strike. The second problem was that the hostile ideological depiction of working miners as the people and pickets as the mob by opponents of the strike was encouraged by the way in which the left separated strikers from scabs. Ironically, it was the left, and not its opponents, that ensured that the people–mob dichotomy dominated the public debate over the strike in a way that eclipsed the "real issues" involved.

NOTES

1. In this chapter, "right" and "left" are used as relative terms within British trade union politics. This political spectrum ranges from supporters of the mixed economy on the right to communists on the left.

2. See Ian MacGregor, *The Enemies Within* (London: Collins, 1986), pp. 127–29; Geoffrey Goodman, *The Miners' Strike* (London: Pluto Press, 1985), p. 30.

3. Martin Adeney and John Lloyd, *The Miners' Strike 1984–5* (London: Routledge and Kegan Paul, 1986), p. 37.

4. Margaret Felicia Kahn, "The National Union of Mineworkers and the Revival of Industrial Militancy in the 1970's," doctoral thesis, University of California at Berkeley, 1984, p. 258.

5. Arthur Scargill, "The New Unionism," *New Left Review* 92 (1975): p. 14.

6. This was made plain in a document leaked to *The Economist* in 1978, which described the elaborate plans the Conservatives had for defeating the miners in a strike. The document, written by future cabinet member Nicholas Ridley, was summarized in "Appomattox or Civil War?" *The Economist*, 27 May 1978, pp. 21–22.

7. Scargill, "The New Unionism," p. 27.

8. See Peggy Kahn, "Coal Not Dole: The British Miners' Strike of 1984–85," *Socialist Review* 93–94, Vol. 17, no. 3–4 (1987): 66.

9. Personal interview, Victor Allen, 18 April 1990.

10. Personal interview, Peggy Kahn, 28–29 March 1989.

11. Kahn, "Coal Not Dole," p. 67.

12. Personal interview, Yorkshire NUM branch official, 12 March 1990.

13. The NCB, which now calls itself British Coal, has still not enforced compulsory redundancies but has relied on lump sum payments and increasingly intrusive, petty, exploitative and "robust" management practices to encourage miners to quit.

14. This tactic was discussed in Ridley's document. See "Appomattox or Civil War?" p. 22.

15. Jonathan and Ruth Winterton, *Coal, Crisis and Conflict* (Manchester, England: Manchester University Press, 1989), pp 56, 57, 59.

16. NUM press release, 26 Jan. 1984.

17. NUM press releases, 19 Feb. 1984, 6 March 1984.

18. *The Times* (London), 25 August 1989, p. 18. About 14,000 miners left the industry during the strike; several hundred of them were sacked after being convicted of offenses committed while picketing.

19. See Winterton, *Coal*, pp. 64–70.

20. Roy Ottey, *The Strike: An Insider's Story* (London: Sidgwick and Jackson, 1985), p. 110.

21. Yorkshire officials had in fact conducted an area ballot three years earlier; a very general motion, authorizing the area officials to take any measure deemed necessary to fight pit closures, including a strike, had been approved by 81 percent of the voters. This ballot, the left said, legitimized the strike. It was, a miner later recalled, like "something out of your past grabbing hold of you by the back of your neck." Personal interview, Yorkshire NUM member, 9 March 1990.

22. Of the areas that held a ballot, only in Northumberland did a majority of 52 percent favor the strike. In the North Derbyshire, North Wales, and Durham areas, ballots in which the majority voted not to strike were ignored. In North Derbyshire, the vote was almost exactly split, while in the other two areas, the majority against striking ranged from 68 to 85 percent. See Ottey, *The Strike*, p. 73.

23. John Saville, "An Open Conspiracy: Conservative Politics and the Miners' Strike 1984–5," *The Socialist Register 1985/86*, Ralph Miliband et al., eds. (London: Merlin, 1986), p. 312.

24. Ibid.

25. Personal interview, Yorkshire NUM pit delegate, 14 May 1990.

26. This distinction is made in Winterton, *Coal*, pp. 75–77. A critical examination of the literature on why the Nottinghamshire miners did

not join the strike is made by Peter Gibbon, "Analysing the British Miners' Strike of 1984–5," *Economy and Society* 17 (May 1988): 171–76.

27. Personal interview, Peggy Kahn, 28–29 March 1989.

28. Eric Booth, "Scabbington Colliery" cartoon, *Yorkshire Miner*, Strike Issue 2, June 1984.

29. For example, see the appeals made in *The Miner*, special issue, 30 June 1984, including L. J. Fisher, "Nothing Without a Struggle," p. 2; Arthur Scargill, "Full Weight of State Will not Defeat Us," p 4.

30. For example, see Jan Stead, *Never the Same Again: Women and the Miners' Strike 1984–85* (London: Women's Press, 1987), pp. 103, 107.

31. Billy Smith, "Nottingham/1984—Scabs—1985," *Durham Striker*, reproduced in *The Nottinghamshire Miner* 6 (September 1985): 4; personal interview, Yorkshire pit delegate, 14 May 1990.

32. Personal interview, Union of Democratic Mineworkers officer, 9 March 1990.

33. Winterton, *Coal*, p. 73.

34. Ian MacGregor, *The Enemies Within* (London: Collins, 1986), p. 219.

35. MacGregor refers to elements among the strikers as "the mob" at least sixteen times. See *The Enemies Within*, pp. 52, 151, 163, 169, 171, 173, 174, 182, 197, 200, 208, 325, 328, 331, 359, 376.

36. Ibid., pp. 327, 269, 199.

37. Ibid., p. 199.

38. Ibid., p. 219.

39. For example, see the cartoon, "As you can see from today's turnout the strike is SOLID," *The Nottinghamshire Miner* 2 (March 1985).

40. Cited in Adeney and Lloyd, *The Miner's Strike*, p. 294.

41. Personal interview, UDM officer, 9 March 1990. The Militant Tendency was an extreme left group within the Labour Party whose leading members have been expelled; WRP stands for Workers Revolutionary Party.

42. Nottinghamshire miner quoted in Adeney and Lloyd, *The Miner's Strike*, p. 264, from an unspecified *Financial Times* reported by Phillip Bassett.

43. Personal interview, UDM associate, 18 May 1990.

44. MacGregor, *The Enemies Within*, p. 187.

45. Allen traces the origin of the flying picket to a dispute in Yorkshire in 1955, although, as he points out, such picketing could not realize its full potential until most miners had cars. Victor L. Allen, *The Militancy of British Miners* (Shipley: Moor Press, 1981), p. 191. Kahn dates flying picketing from 1969 in "The National Union of Mineworkers," p. 255.

46. Personal interview, UDM Nottinghamshire area official, 9 April 1990.

47. The strike call was defeated by 193,985 to 41,322 votes. According to Allen:

The national officials who framed the ballot paper lumped the wages and hours questions together. The acceptance of one was dependent upon accepting the other. . . . This was a devious but well-known way of getting an unsatisfactory offer accepted. It was known that a majority of the miners would not wish to reject the wages offer which affected them all in order to get an improvement in the working hours of a small minority. (*Militancy*, p. 159)

Also see Scargill, "The New Unionism," pp. 10–11. It can be noted that the tactic described by Allen was mirrored by the left in the national strike ballot of October 1982 in an effort to link wage militancy to opposition to closures.

48. Ottey, *The Strike*, pp. 92–113; Michael Crick, *Scargill and the Miners* (Harmondsworth: Penguin, 1985), pp. 103–6.

49. The morning shift abandoned work to reach the meeting en masse and vote against the strike. Personal interview, UDM Nottinghamshire branch official, 9 April 1990.

50. Joe Gormley, *Battered Cherub* (London: Hamish Hamilton, 1982).

51. Victor Allen, personal interview, 18 April 1990.

52. For example, see Crick, *Scargill*, p. 186.

53. Raphael Samuel et al., *The Enemy Within: Pit Villages and the Miners' Strike of 1984–5* (London: Routledge and Kegan Paul, 1986), pp. 6–12.

54. The People of Thurcroft, *Thurcroft: A Village and the Miners' Strike*, copyright Peter Gibbon and David Steyne (London: Spokesman, 1986), p. 7. See also Gibbon, "Analysing the British Miners' Strike," pp. 150–52.

55. The People of Thurcroft, p. 105.

56. Ibid., p. 107.

57. Adeney and Lloyd, *The Miners' Strike*, p. 94.

58. Personal interview, Yorkshire NUM member, 9 March 1990.

59. Personal interviews: Yorkshire NUM member, 9 March 1990; former NUM member, 15 May 1990; Ken Ambler, *A Coalfield in Chaos* (Bridlington, England: Ken Ambler, n.d.), p. 90.

60. North Yorkshire Women Against Pit Closures, *Strike 84–85* (Leeds, 1985), p. 41.

61. The Wintertons have compiled statistics that show that there was a trend for early strikebreakers to live outside the striking communities. See Winterton, *Coal*, pp. 174, 180.

62. M. McGuire, "The Scab Watch Team," in *A Year of Our Lives Hatfield Main a Colliery Community in the Great Coal Strike of 1984/85* ("This book has been produced by the people of Hatfield Main Colliery"), David John Douglas, ed. (England: Hooligan Press, 1986).

63. Ibid.

64. Ibid.

65. For example, see the unsigned piece on "The Fate of Scabs," in *A Year of Our Lives Hatfield Main*.

66. MacGregor, *The Enemies Within*, p. 357.

67. Personal interview, Yorkshire NUM member, 12 March 1990.

68. The People of Thurcroft, p. 248.

69. Personal interview, Yorkshire NUM member, 9 March 1990.

70. Personal interview, Yorkshire NUM member, 15 May 1990.

71. Personal interview, UDM associate, 15 May 1990.

72. "The Fate of Scabs,"

73. Personal interview, Yorkshire NUM member, 15 May 1990.

74. For example, see Jack Taylor et al., "Breakaways Merely Weaken Our Common Strength—Area Officials," *Yorkshire Miner* 81 (August 1985): 1.

75. "What Arthur Scargill Thinks of You," *Nottinghamshire Miner* 1 (February 1985), n.p.

CHAPTER 7

The Dilemma of Democratization in Eastern Europe

The ideological use of the people and the mob in Europe reached its height in the interwar period with the rise of fascism. The subsequent victory of the allies in World War II and the establishment of democratic corporatism in the West meant that political analysis and rhetoric based on this dichotomy went into decline. The distinction between the people and the mob no longer formed an integral component of a major ideology in Europe but was used only in response to exceptional circumstances.

The account of the miners' strike has shown that the breakdown of the postwar corporatist consensus in Britain since the Conservatives gained power in 1979 could result in conflicts in which the people–mob dichotomy was used in ideological debate. But the use of this dichotomy was not so much a fixed feature of the ideologies involved as a temporary convenience, a contingent reaction to heightened conflict. It is possible, however, that the use of the people–mob dichotomy may become re-established not in the West but rather in the ideologies developing in the new democracies of Eastern Europe.

"Democracy" and "market economy" are often used interchangeably by Western politicians and journalists to describe the goals of reformist governments in Eastern Europe. This perspective tends to assume that the political and economic changes that have been taking place in Poland, Czechoslovakia, Hungary, Romania, Bulgaria, Yugoslavia, in former East Germany, and Albania can be reduced to a simple graph in which movement from dictatorship to democracy is directly proportional to the movement from a communist to a liberal-capitalist system. Of course, the liberal-right in the West has an obvious domestic ideological agenda in promoting the view that political freedom and laissez-faire capitalism are synonymous.[1] But even if the idea that these terms are essentially the same is dismissed as propaganda, it is hard to deny that the changes in Eastern Europe, in their early stages, have approximately followed the line of such a graph.

It may be that the simple linear relationship between democratic political reform and "economic democracy," that is, liberal capitalism, has run its course. These two aspects of change in Eastern Europe do not have a mutual affinity but rather engender contradictory ideological imperatives on the new political elites. In particular, there is a contradiction between the political need to gain or retain popular legitimacy by making communalistic or nationalistic appeals to the people on the one hand, and the economic need to replace the idea of the people with a liberal concept of a competitive society of individuals or pluralist groups on the other.

THE DILEMMA

To overthrow the dictatorships of Eastern Europe, the unifying ideology of the people was necessary. To institute reforms in East Europe that combine political democracy with economic liberalism, a divisive ideology in which it is assumed to be right and proper that individuals and groups engage in economic competition in the market must replace the ideology of the people. However, the ideology of the people, once generated, cannot easily be dispelled. It cannot be assumed that after the dictators have been overthrown, the potential for mass mobilization around the ideology of the people will simply disappear. On the contrary, the rapid development of democratic reform has provided an institutional framework that ensures that this type of ideology will continue to be encouraged, as it provides not only an established doctrine in a time of flux, but also a mechanism through which politicians may gain mass popularity and political power. The core of the dilemma that faces Eastern Europe, therefore, is that while there may be economic reasons to develop a pluralist system, political power is secured not by pluralism but by populism. This is particularly true, given that a capitalist economic structure is still in its earliest stages of development, while a democratic political structure is already largely in place.

OPPOSITION TO REFORMED COMMUNISTS

One of the consequences of this dilemma is evident in the democratic election of governments composed of reformed Communist Party members and in the ideology used to justify the continuing protests against them by their political adversaries. Opponents of reformed communist governments have condemned them as opportunists associated with the fallen dictators. They have suggested that a half-revolution has taken place, one that has not yet reached the stage of the revolutions in other countries where governments with truly non-communist regimes have been elected.[2] Underlying this argument is the teleological assumption that the revolution in East Europe can be completed only by the complete removal of all former communists. But this assumption is somewhat misleading. The East European revolutions were not simply about the replacement of communism with capitalism but were also an affirmation of belief in the people. In appealing to the people, the reformed communists did not subvert the revolution but rather adopted one of its ideological aspects as their own. The electoral success of the reformed communists, therefore, was not an indication of the failure of the revolution but was one of its contradictory consequences.

In 1989, the communist regime in East Germany responded to mass protests with force. The subsequent clashes between demonstrators and the police were described by the communists as the confrontation between the mob and the people. Thus, the state press agency said of the demonstrations of October 7–8, 1989: "The violence caused by hooligans who were provoked by the international media was stopped by the People's Police and order was restored."[3]

This explanation of civil conflict was repeated sixteen months later in Albania. Sabrio Godu of the Albanian Workers Party responded to the demonstrations of February 20, 1991, by arguing that the police response might equally have come from the people themselves: "There must be more trust in the people. The people do not want murderers, vagabonds, and criminals. Every one citizen would be ready to give help within his abilities to isolate such people."[4] Similar propaganda was put out by the other communist regimes in Eastern Europe who faced mass demonstrations.

The response of the protesters was to reject their designation as the mob by affirming the opposite. Thus, the protestors in East Germany chanted, "We are the people! We are the people!" at the police.[5] Similarly in Romania, where Ceausescu had branded the protesters as "hooligans," they sang: "We're the people. Down with the dictator!"[6] As this ideological confrontation between communist regimes and the mass protestors suggests, while the demonstrators refuted the specific charge that they were the mob, they did not challenge the dichotomy between "people" and "mob" per se, so much as redefine it as a division between the people, by which they meant themselves, and their oppressors, by which they meant the government.

Before the successful election campaigns of the reformed communist parties, the anti-communist protesters' self-identification as being at one with the people was premised on a simple and unproblematic association between civic virtue and the majority. However, the votes subsequently gained by communists in Romania after the election of the National Salvation Front under Ion Iliescu, in Serbia after the election of the leader of the Socialist Party of Serbia Slobodan Milosevic, and in Albania before the elected government of the Albanian Workers Party resigned in June 1991 put their opponents in a frustrating position. It would seem that the people had been misled into voting for the political functionaries of the old regimes. To retain their claim to be the people, therefore, the opponents of the new democratic regimes were forced to reformulate the meaning of the term to explain their loss at the polls. The way in which this was done illustrates how ideological imperatives in East Europe link the concept of the people to that of the mob.

Two years before civil war broke out in Yugoslavia, Tomaz Mastnak, a Slovenian intellectual opposed to the rise of Milosevic in Serbia, said: "A new form of psychology, rooted mainly in a peculiar form of national consciousness, supported by political primitivism and incapable of any rational argumentation, is spreading over the whole country."[7] In this situation:

> It is true that Milosevic enjoys great support amongst the Serbs, but his sympathisers do not come from one particular class. They are a temporary assortment of the population—nationalist, intolerant, aggressive, irrational, manipulated and unaware of their own interests. When saying that Milosevic is 'supported by the people', we must bear in mind that recent Serbian politics has turned the people into a Party and state mob.
> . . . The congeniality between the political despots and the revolutionary mob reveals that the neo-orthodox, authoritarian Communist Party is merely the best organised mob, its political elite.[8]

While Mastnak provided a sophisticated social analysis of events in Yugoslavia, the underlying structure of his argument is typical of the way in which activists opposed to the newly elected regimes have made a transition from viewing the majority as the people to interpreting them as the mob. Nonetheless, opposition activists have attempted to retain their claim to be the people by modifying the meaning of both terms. The first modification has been to argue that the people cannot be manipulated. This quality of the people is assumed to be directly related to levels of education and to urban rather than rural living conditions. In contrast, the mob can be manipulated easily. A second modification has been to redefine the people as a physically mobilized group and thus to identify them with an actual mass gathering rather than with the abstract calculation of political views of the majority through elections. From this perspective, a crowd, through its appearance of being the majority, and not the majority of voters, has the political authority to determine the legitimacy of a government.

These modifications to the people–mob dichotomy might appear to be contradictory. Primitive, irrational, and manipulated political behavior may be identified with less educated sectors of the population, and yet to describe the masses as a mob in this way is to draw on a characterization that is historically, and to some extent justifiably, related to the idea of the crowd. But whatever its theoretical shortcomings, the redefinition of the people and the mob has been ideologically effective. It has allowed the opposition to retain its capacity for political action through mass mobilization and to claim that this action is legitimate. The distinction between those who have been manipulated and those who have not allows the rhetoric of the people to be retained. At the same time, this social category is defined in terms that are epitomized by students and intellectuals, the two groups that have provided the highest levels of opposition support, while the low level of rural support for the opposition can be discounted as being the result of manipulation.

To call this redefinition of the people and the mob ideologically effective, however, is not to say that it is unproblematic. The newly elected reformed communist governments have made three responses in an attempt to retain their popularity. The first response has been to describe the protesters as the mob attacking the government of the people, just as the previous regimes had done—although this time with a much greater claim to represent the people. The second response has been to oppose the large urban protests with counter-demonstrations, although these have been comparatively difficult to organize, given that the reformed communists' greatest strength is in their dispersed rural constituency. The third response has been to characterize the protesters as elitists who view the people as the mob.[9] These three responses can be

illustrated in Romania and Albania, where reformed communists gained
a majority vote in free elections in 1990 and 1991, with their highest
levels of support coming from smaller towns and rural areas, while the
greatest opposition came from the larger cities. After these elections, both
governments faced continuing urban demonstrations.

Romania

In the aftermath of an anti-government riot in Bucharest on June 13,
1990, several thousand Romanian miners were bussed into the capital to
defend the government and attack the protesters, who had been camping
in University Square. A little over a year later, miners would themselves
be demonstrating against the government, but in 1990, they provided it
with effective and violent support. On June 15, President Ion Iliescu
thanked them:

> Dear miners, I thank you very much for your feelings of solidarity and
> for everything you have done these past few days, and in general, for your
> attitude of civic awareness. Your example was full of encouragement for
> all people of good faith who want the progress of Romanian society.
>   We were faced with an attempted coup by a force of extremist, rightist
> elements, a coup with iron-guardist and fascist character. . . . [They drew
> on] all kinds of peripheral malcontent elements or parasitic elements of our
> society, whom they were supporting for the last two months in University
> Square in a climate of moral misery and corruption, and whom they
> fed, . . . paid, and drugged in order to put them in a state of euphoria
> and fanaticism for such moments. We are dealing here with a broader
> scenario of European proportions; there was a joint alliance of right-wing
> forces which started from the presumption that right-wing forces in all
> East European countries should come to power. . . .
>   We should maintain a spirit of mobilization and struggle of all those
> determined to defend Romanian democracy, which is serving the many,
> the people. This is not a democracy which serves the rich or those who
> become rich at the expense of the people.
>   We know that we can rely on you. When necessary we will call on
> you. . . . I extend to you wishes for maximum results and efficiency
> at work.[10]

The National Salvation Front had been confronted with continuing protests
since its members seized control of the government after the mass revolt
of December 1989. They had responded by attempting to discredit their
opponents as the mob. Thus, the protesters were labeled as vagabonds

(*golani*) or described as unemployed, knife-wielding former prisoners bribed to riot by sinister foreigners.[11] In his speech, Iliescu can be seen to have expanded on this characterization of the protesters and contrasted it with a dichotomous depiction of the miners as the people.

Iliescu established the legitimacy of the miners' attack on the protesters by defining it as a defense of a popular government, one that represented the majority of the population—"the many, the people." Implicit was the idea that the miners were of the people; they were drawn from the people and exemplified their virtues of "civic awareness" and engaging in productive and useful work with "maximum results and efficiency." The character of the miners, their social background, and the value of their work to Romanian society was brought into relief by drawing a contrast drawn between them and the protesters, whose social composition, political aims, and reasons for engaging in the riot were combined to explain why their demonstration was illegitimate and needed to be suppressed.

The protesters were said to be made up of two elements. The first was a "peripheral" minority of the population, one that was separated from the majority because its members did not contribute toward the prosperity and progress of society as a whole but were "parasites" on it. These "malcontents" were ethically as well as economically separated from the majority by Iliescu; they existed "in a climate of moral misery." The second element Iliescu identified among the protestors were the agitators—extremists engaged in an international right-wing conspiracy. It was this element that was said to have incited the former to riot on June 13. In contrast to the public-spirited actions of the miners, the rioters were said to have been given material inducements; they were "fed, . . . paid, and drugged." Their normal mental state was transformed into an extreme and emotional one; they were rendered "fanatical" and "euphoric." In sum, just as the picture of the miners epitomizes the idea of the people, so the picture of the demonstrators in University Square epitomizes the opposing idea of the mob.

The context of Iliescu's address suggests why he chose to present the conflict in such a manner. The six-week demonstration in University Square and the riot on June 13 presented a challenge to two of the bases of state legitimacy. There was first the immediate physical challenge to the control of government institutions through the attempts to enter and burn the Romanian parliament, Interior Ministry and television station. Second, there was the more intangible but no less threatening challenge to Iliescu's claim to represent the people. This second challenge explains Iliescu's use of the miners rather than the military to attack the demonstrators. The military had the physical capacity to defend the institutions of government and disperse the immediate physical threat of the protestors, but the miners combined this capacity with the potential to symbolize the people. The picture Iliescu drew of the miners was designed to suggest this idea; the picture that he drew of the demonstrators was designed to reinforce it. The majority was separated from the minority, workers from parasites, public-spirited actions in the national interest from international conspiracy, bribery, and crowd irrationalism.

Albania

The Albanian Workers Party responded to the protests before and after the 1991 election that briefly confirmed it in power in a manner very similar to the National Salvation Front in Romania. Thus, speaking shortly before the election, Prime Minister Alia stated:

> A crowd of dissatisfied people, taking leave of all sense of reason and logic, committed acts of vandalism. . . . It has now emerged with total clarity that antidemocratic forces have a precise strategy. They want to destroy Albania. . . .
>
> These forces incite and urge people in pursuit of political interests. Their aim is to estrange the masses from the power of the people, a cynical game with the feelings of the people. . . .
>
> I call on everyone to take their destiny into their own hands. Today is the day to show who is a patriot who loves Albania at heart, who suffers in toil and sheds sweat, and who really loves democracy.[12]

Alia thus contrasted the mob with the people. Both concepts are characterized in ways that are typical. The mob is described in terms that combine a systematic conspiracy with an irrational crowd; the people are identified through the description of their virtuous participation in hard work. Alia's nationalist call to lovers of Albania reinforces the appeal to the people.

The success of the Albanian Workers Party in the elections of 1991 did not prevent the protests from continuing or extinguish the protesters' claim to be the people. Ultimately, this led to the resignation of the government. In its initial response, however, the government publicized two arguments. First, it claimed that the protesters slandered the peasants and others who had voted for the government as stupid and gullible, where in fact they were the finest of the people. Second, the government argued that mass demonstrations against it were contrived to appear to be made up of the people, where in fact they were made up of an "irritated mob" of thieves and vandals.[13] In this way the protesters—that is, the mob— were said to have conspired to mislead the people. Thus, it was claimed in the Albanian parliament:

> In all cases of illegal gatherings beginning since February 20, 1991, the organisers line up children and women in front of the mobs. The aim is for the police not to attack, and if it attacks them under the law, then the press organs, speakers, etc. have attempted to raise the people against the police and one cannot say they have failed to attain the goal.[14]

THE FUTURE OF EASTERN EUROPE AND ITS PAST

At a 1991 anti-government demonstration in Poland, a petition was circulated that advocated " a true parliamentary democracy and market economy" while calling for an end to "growing unemployment, low wages, and the crazy growth of prices of apartments and rents."[15] This petition neatly summarizes the contradictory economic demands made on the Polish government under Lech Walesa, as well as the other governments in Eastern Europe. The West, with its comparative material prosperity, provides an economic as well as a political model, yet the short-term consequences of attempting to restructure the East European economies are bound to affect most of the population adversely. Redundancies made in the name of profit, monetary devaluation, and the ending of price fixing on housing and basic commodities are all examples of the immediate negative consequences of liberal economic reform.

Industrial opposition to this type of reform has been considerable. In the short-term aftermath of political democratization there have been several major strikes, including rail strikes in former East Germany and Romania and a miners' strike in Bulgaria. Meanwhile, the political opponents of East Europe's new governments, naturally enough, have construed the economic reforms as an attack on the people. For example, Vladimir Merciar, the prime minister of Bratislavia in Czechoslovakia, responded to the idea of returning confiscated land to its original owners:

> Who will pay for it? In November I saw the simple people standing in the street. You were from the factories, you were from the offices, and you were shouting that you want to have a better life. Why should you now, today, pay out of your own pockets for mistakes you did not make?[16]

Therefore, not only do politicians in Eastern Europe have a political imperative to appeal to the people and an economic imperative not to, but the widespread aspiration to have a standard of living comparable to the West is not seen in the context of the economic sacrifices demanded by liberal-capitalism.

This dilemma might be resolved in various ways. In Hungary, for example, the government allowed incremental democratic reform before the revolts of 1989. As a consequence, the unifying ideology of the people has played a comparatively minor role in the opposition to communist rule.[17] In Poland, a pattern of elections similar to Walesa's replacement of Mazowiecki, in which populist promises are followed by liberal policies, might conceivably allow it to develop a liberal economic system. However, it is also possible that other politicians may respond to these dilemmas by adopting the political forms found in Eastern Europe during the interwar period—the most recent and, in some instances, the only period of modern national independence before the communists gained control. During this time, the ideology of most governments and various opposition movements reflected an adherence to "integral nationalism" and a form of corporatism akin to fascism.[18] This type of ideology is in a position to resolve the dilemmas facing Eastern Europe in three ways. First, the general repudiation of socialism and the reluctance to accept the austerities of capitalist restructuring can be resolved by the promise of a "third way," that is, corporatist economics. Second, the economic policy of fascist and authoritarian forms of corporatism is based on the maintenance of the ideology of the people rather than its breakdown. Third, the conflicts that may occur under such a system can be resolved by repression in the name of the people against the mob.

The shift in the idea of the people to reflect the ideology of nationalism in Eastern Europe since the revolutions of 1989 may be the first step in the reconstruction of past political forms. The role of the people in radical European ideologies has been associated with two manifest objectives. The first has been the aim of human emancipation, the release from oppression, and the extension of the franchise and of political liberties. The second has been the aim of national fulfillment, cultural expression, and the development of a homogeneous society within ethnically defined national borders. In the nineteenth century, the humanist concept of the people that had previously predominated began to give way to a concept with nationalist associations. This revised concept of the people was reflected in the corporatist ideologies of the interwar regimes in Eastern Europe.

This shift in the ideological significance of the people in Europe between the French Revolution and World War II is reflected, albeit in a much shorter time frame, in the aftermath of the revolutions in Eastern

Europe. At the outset of the anti-communist revolt, the people were seen as emancipating themselves from oppressive and dictatorial rule, and pursuing political freedom. The collapse of the oppressors, however, has often been followed by the redefinition of the people as national units (which are often actually subnational or transnational units). Hence, the idea of the revolt of the people of Eastern Europe has been replaced by the idea of the revolt of the peoples of Eastern Europe.

This redefinition of the people has been accompanied by a shift from political to social groups perceived as the enemies of the people. The opponents of the people in the emerging nationalist ideologies are no longer the communists; they are other groups, other peoples. It is here that the idea of the people may become linked to that of the mob.

NOTES

1. An amusing example is Margaret Thatcher's 1989 speech to the Conservative Party conference, in which she modestly took the credit for East Europe's revolt.

2. For example, see "The Timisoara Proclamation," *East European Reporter* 4 (1990): 32–35.

3. "Security Forces Storm Protesters in East Germany," *New York Times*, 9 October 1989, p. A6.

4. "Party Representatives Hold Radio Discussion," *Foreign Broadcast Information Service Daily Report East Europe* (hereafter referred to as *FBIS-EEU*), 21 February 1991, p. 6.

5. "Security Forces Storm Protesters," p. A1.

6. Gail Kligman, "Reclaiming the Public: A Reflection on Creating Civil Society in Romania," *East European Politics and Societies* 4 (1990): 407.

7. Tomaz Mastnak, "No Rationale for the Survival of Yugoslavia?" *East European Reporter* 3, No. 3 (1989): 48.

8. Ibid., p. 147.

9. The protesters, of course, reject this third argument by arguing that the manipulation practiced by the new leaders demonstrate that they regard the bulk of the population as the mob. However, the problem in making this claim public is that it is potentially self-defeating. Those accused of manipulation can point to the low opinion of the political and intellectual capacities of the people that is implicit in such an argument, while insofar as these politicians are manipulative, they will invariably refer to the bulk of society as the people in public, regardless of what they think of them in private. However, Silviu Brucan, of Romania's National Salvation Front, provides an example of a politician who held different private and public views of the Romanian population, which—with the charming naivete of a participant in a fledging democracy—he rashly described to two

journalists from *The Independent*. "In the post-communist society he hopes to build," the journalists wrote indignantly in an article published both in London and in the opposition newspaper, *Romania Libera*, "there will be only two classes: clever people and stupid people. Ideally, clever people will be the rulers, and stupid people will happily vote for their masters in exchange for some basic comforts." The journalists said Brucan had confided to them: "I am telling this to the intellectuals of *The Independent*, not to the people of Romania. They would not understand. We shall have to present these ideas in a popular way." See Imre Karacs and Victoria Clark, "Brucan Dreams of Brain Power," *The Independent* (London) 29 January 1990, p. 8. See also Silviu Brucan's letter, *The Independent*, 3 February 1990, p. 17. Brucan subsequently resigned. See Patricia Clough, "Brucan Resigns, Condemning 'Opportunism,' " *The Independent*, 5 February 1990, p. 8.

10. *The Independent*, 21 June 1990, p. 10.

11. Ian Traynor, "Romania Warns Off Street Protesters," *Guardian* (London), 20 February 1990, p. 8.

12. "Alia Takes Over Direction of Matters of State," *FBIS-EEU*, 21 February 1991, pp. 4–5.

13. "People's Assembly Session Discusses Issues," *FBIS-EEU*, 30 April 1991, pp. 1–2.

14. Ibid., p. 1. Compare "Interior Ministry Warns of 'Fascist Forces,' " *FBIS-EEU*, 15 February 1991, p. 2; "Council of Ministers Communique," *FBIS-EEU*, 21 February 1991, p. 3.

15. "May Day Demonstrators Protest Against Government," *FBIS-EEU*, 1 May 1991, p 22.

16. "Merciar Criticizes Bill on Return of Property," *FBIS-EEU*, 19 February 1991, p. 29. A further case in point is seen in the "populist" 1990 election campaign of Walesa. Ironically, Walesa's policies once in power have reverted to the liberal restructuring of his unpopular predecessor, Mazowiecki. See "Poland: The Kaczynski Card," *East European Newsletter* 5 (2 April 1991): 5–7.

17. See Janina Frentzel-Zagorska, "Civil Society in Poland and Hungary," *Soviet Studies* 42 (1990): 759–777.

18. See Joseph Rothschild, *East Central Europe between the Two World Wars*, vol. 9 of *A History of East Central Europe*, Peter F. Sugar and Donald W. Treadgold, eds. (Seattle: University of Washington Press, 1974); John A. Armstrong, "Collaborationism in World War Two," *Journal of Modern History* 40 (1968): 396–410; Andrew C. Janos, "The One-Party State and Social Mobilization," in *Authoritarian Politics in Modern Society*, Samuel P. Huntington and Clement H. Moore, eds. (New York: Basic Books, 1970); Antony Polonsky, *The Little Dictators* (London: Routledge and Kegan Paul, 1975); Gilbert Oddo, *Slovakia and its People* (New York: Spellar, 1960); *Nationalism in Eastern Europe*, Peter F. Sugar and Ivo J. Lederer, eds. (Seattle: University of Washington Press, 1969).

Bibliography

Adeney, Martin, and John Lloyd. *The Miners' Strike 1984–5*. London: Routledge and Kegan Paul, 1986.

Allen, Victor L. *The Militancy of British Miners*. Shipley, England: Moor Press, 1981.

———. *Trade Union Leadership*. Cambridge, Mass.: Harvard University Press, 1957.

Ambler, Ken. *A Coalfield in Chaos*. Bridlington, England: Ken Ambler, n.d.

"Appomattox or Civil War?" *The Economist*, 27 May 1978, pp. 21–22.

Arendt, Hannah. *The Origins of Totalitarianism*, 3rd ed. New York: Harcourt, Brace and World, 1966.

———. *The Human Condition*. Chicago: University of Chicago Press, 1958.

Armstrong, John A. "Collaborationism in World War Two: The Integral Nationalist Variant in Eastern Europe." *Journal of Modern History* 40 (1968): 396–410.

"As you can see from today's turnout the strike is SOLID" (cartoon). *The Nottinghamshire Miner* 2 (March 1985): n.p.

Bakunin, Michael. *Bakunin on Anarchy*, Translated and edited by Sam Dolgoff. London: George Allen and Unwin, 1973.

Barrès, Maurice. *Le Roman de L'énergie nationale: les déracinés*. Paris: Librairie Plon, 1922.

Bauer, Otto. "Fascism." In *Austro-Marxism*, edited by Tom Bottomore and Patrick Goode. Oxford: Clarendon Press, 1978.

Beetham, David, editor. *Marxists in Face of Fascism*. Manchester, England: Manchester University Press, 1983.

———. "From Socialism to Fascism in the Work of Robert Michels. II: The

Fascist Ideologue." *Political Studies* 25 (1977): 161–81.

Beier, A. L. *Masterless Men. The Vagrancy Problem in England 1560–1640.* London: Methuen, 1985.

Bellamy, Edward. *Equality.* New York: D. Appleton, 1897.

Bernstein, Herman. *The Truth about "The Protocols of Zion."* New York: Ktav, 1971.

Best, Geoffrey. "Review of *The Making of the English Working Class.*" *The Historical Journal* 8 (1965): 271–281.

Booth, Eric. "Scabbington Colliery" (cartoon). *Yorkshire Miner* 2 (June 1984).

Bottomore, Tom. "Lumpenproletariat." In *A Dictionary of Marxist Thought*, edited by Tom Bottomore. Oxford: Basil Blackwell, 1983.

Botz, Gehard. "The Changing Pattern of Social Support for Austrian National Socialism (1918-1945)." In *Who Were the Fascists*, edited by Stein Vgelvik Larson et al., pp. 202–25. Bergen, Norway: Universitetsforlager, 1980.

Bovenkerk, Frank. "The Rehabilitation of the Rabble; How and Why Marx and Engels Wrongly Depicted the Lumpenproletariat as a Reactionary Force." *Netherlands Journal of Sociology* 20 (April 1984): 13–41.

Brucan, Silviu. Letter to the Editor. *The Independent* (London). February 3, 1990, p. 17.

Burke, Edmund. *Reflections on the Revolution in France.* Edited by Conor Cruise O'Brien. Harmondsworth, England: Penguin, 1982.

———. *Burke's Thoughts on the Cause of the Present Discontents.* London: Macmillan, 1902.

Caspard, Pierre. "Aspects de la lutte des classes en 1848: le recrutement de la garde nationale mobile." *Revue Historique* 511 (July 1974): 81–106.

de Castro, J. Paul. *The Gordon Riots.* London: Oxford University Press, 1926.

Chalmers, Douglas A. "Corporatism and Comparative Politics." *New Directions in Comparative Politics*, edited by Howard J. Wiarda, pp. 56–79. Boulder, Colo.: Westview, 1985.

Childers, Thomas. *The Nazi Voter.* Chapel Hill, N.C.: University of North Carolina Press, 1983.

Clough, Patricia. "Brucan Resigns, Condemning 'Opportunism.' " *The Independent* (London). 5 February 1990, p. 8.

Cohn, Norman. *Warrant for Genocide: The Myth of the Jewish World Conspiracy and the Protocols of the Elders of Zion.* New York: Harper and Row, 1967.

Colquhoun, Patrick. *A Treatise on the Police of the Metropolis.* London: Joseph Mawman, in the Poultry, successor to Mr. Dillys, 1800.

Conrad, Joseph. *The Secret Agent.* London: Penguin, 1963.

Converse, Philip E. "The Nature of Belief Systems in Mass Publics." In *Ideology and Discontent*, edited by David E. Apter. London: Macmillan, 1964.

Cottrell, Allin. *Social Classes in Marxist Theory.* London: Routledge and Kegan

Paul, 1984.

Coughlin, Charles E. *"Am I an Anti-Semite?"* Royal Oak, Mich.: C. E. Couglin, 1939.

————. *A Series of Lectures on Social Justice*. Royal Oak, Mich.: Radio League of the Little Flower, 1935.

————. *Eight Lectures on Labor, Capital and Justice*. Royal Oak, Mich.: Radio League of the Little Flower, 1934.

————. *Eight Discourses on the Gold Standard*. Royal Oak, Mich.: Radio League of the Little Flower, 1933.

Crick, Michael. *Scargill and the Miners*. Harmondsworth, England: Penguin, 1985.

Cuza, Alexandru C. "The Science of Anti-Semitism." In *For My Legionaries*, edited by Corneliu Zelea Codreanu. Madrid: Editura "Libertatea," 1976, pp. 37–43.

Darwin, Charles. *The Descent of Man, and Selection in Relation to Sex*. London: John Murray, 1871.

Deak, Istvan. "Hungary." In *The European Right: A Historical Profile*, edited by Hans Rogger and Eugen Weber, pp. 364–407. Berkeley: University of California Press, 1965.

Diamant, Alfred. *Austrian Catholics and the First Republic*. Princeton: Princeton University Press, 1960.

Douglas, Clifford Hugh. *The Monopoly of Credit*. London: Eyre and Spottiswoode, 1937.

Draper, Hal. *Karl Marx's Theory of Revolution*, 2 vols. New York: Monthly Review Press, 1977.

Dubiel, Helmut. "The Specter of Populism," translated by Steven Stottenberg. *Berkeley Journal of Sociology* 31 (1986): 79–91.

Durkheim, Emile. *The Division of Labor in Society*, translated by George Simpson. New York: Macmillan, 1933.

Eckart, Dietrich. *Der Bolschervismus von Moses bis Lenin: Zweigesprach zwischen Adolf Hitler und mir*. Munich: Hoheneicheu-Verlag, 1924.

Engels, Frederick. Introduction to Marx, Karl, *The Class Struggles in France 1848–1850*. New York: International Publishers, 1964.

————. *The Housing Question*. New York: International Publishers, 1935.

"The Fate of Scabs." In *A Year of Our Lives Hatfield Main A Colliery Community in the great coal strike of 1984/85*, "This book has been produced by the people of Hatfield Main Colliery," edited by David John Douglas. England: Hooligan Press, 1986.

Finlay, John L. *Social Credit*. Montreal: McGill-Queens University Press, 1972.

Fisher, L. J. "Nothing Without a Struggle." *The Miner*. Special issue, 30 June 1984, p. 2.

Foreign Broadcast Information Service Daily Report East Europe (FBIS-EEU). 15 February 1991, 19 February 1991, 21 February 1991, 30 April 1991,

1 May 1991.

Foucault, Michel. *Discipline and Punish*, translated by Alan Sheridan. New York: Vintage Books, Random House, 1979.

Fregier, H.-A. *Des classes dangereuses de la population dans les grandes villes, et des moyens de les rendre meilleures*, 2 vols. Paris: J.-B. Baillière, 1840.

Frentzel-Zagorska, Janina. "Civil Society in Poland and Hungary." *Soviet Studies* 42 (1990): 759–77.

Geary, Dick. *European Labour Protest 1848–1939*. London: Croom Helm, 1981.

Geiger, Robert L. "Democracy and the Crowd: The Social History of an Idea in France and Italy, 1890–1914." *Societas* 7 (1977): 47–71.

Gibbon, Peter. "Analysing the British Miners' Strike of 1984–5." *Economy and Society* 17 (1988): 139–94.

Glaus, Beat. "The National Front in Switzerland." In *Who Were the Fascists?* edited by Stein Vgelvik Larson et al., Bergen, Norway: Universitetsforlager, 1980, pp. 467–78.

Goncourt, Edmond. *Journal des Goncourt 1870–71*. Paris: Bibliothèque Charpentier, 1890.

Goodman, Geoffrey. *The Miners' Strike*. London: Pluto Press, 1985.

Gormley, Joe. *Battered Cherub*. London: Hamish Hamilton, 1982.

Gramsci, Antonio. *Selections from Political Writings 1921–1926*. Translated by Quintin Hoare. New York: International Publishers, 1978.

———. *The Modern Prince*. New York: International Publishers, 1978.

Guerin, Daniel. *Fascism and Big Business*, translated by Frances and Mason Merrill. New York: Pioneer Publishers, 1939.

Hall, Stuart. "The 'Political' and the 'Economic' in Marx's Theory of Classes." In *Class and Class Structure*, edited by Alan Hunt. London: Lawrence and Wishart, 1977.

Hamilton, Richard F. *Who Voted for Hitler?* Princeton: Princeton University Press, 1982.

Hargrave, John Gordon. *Summer Time Ends*. London: Constable, 1935.

Harrison, Mark. *Crowds and History: Mass Phenomena in English Towns, 1790–1835*. Cambridge: Cambridge University Press, 1988.

———. "The Ordering of the Urban Environment: Time, Work and the Occurrence of Crowds 1790–1835." *Past and Present* 110 (1986): 134–68.

Hayes, Peter. "*Utopia* and the Lumpenproletariat: Marx's Reasoning in *The Eighteenth Brumaire of Louis Bonaparte*." *Review of Politics* 50 (1988): 445–65.

Hegel, Georg W. F. *Hegel's Philosophy of Right*, translated by T. M. Knox. London: Oxford University Press, 1967.

Heyl, John D. "Hitler's Economic Thought: A Reappraisal." *Central European History* 6 (1973): 83–96.

Hill, Christopher. "The Many Headed Monster." In *Change and Continuity in Seventeenth Century England*, edited by Christopher Hill, pp. 181–220. London: Wiedenfeld and Nicolson, 1974.

Hitler, Adolf. *Mein Kampf*, translated by Ralph Manheim. London: Hutchinson, 1969.

———. *The Speeches of Adolf Hitler April 1922–August 1939*, 2 vols., translated by Norman H. Baynes. New York: Howard Fertig, 1969.

Holton, Robert J. "The Crowd in History: Some Problems in Theory and Method." *Social History* 3 (May 1978): 219–33.

Janos, Andrew C. "The One-Party State and Social Mobilization: East Europe Between the Wars." In *Authoritarian Politics in Modern Society*, edited by Samuel P. Huntington and Clement H. Moore. New York: Basic Books, 1970.

Jessop, Bob. "Corporatism, Parliamentarism and Social Democracy." In *Trends Toward Corporatist Intermediation*, edited by Philippe C. Schmitter and Gerhard Lehmbruch, pp. 185–202. Beverly Hills, Calif.: Sage, 1979.

The Jewish Peril: Protocols of the Learned Elders of Zion, 3rd ed. London: The Britons, 1920.

Kahn, Margaret Felicia. "The National Union of Mineworkers and the Revival of Industrial Militancy in the 1970's." Ph.D. thesis. University of California at Berkeley, 1984.

Kahn, Peggy. "Coal Not Dole: The British Miners' Strike of 1984–85." *Socialist Review* 93–94, Vol. 17, No. 3–4 (1987): 57–88.

Karacs, Imre and Victoria Clark. "Brucan Dreams of Brain Power." *The Independent* (London). 29 January 1990, p. 8.

Keynes, John Maynard. *The General Theory of Employment Interest and Money*. New York: Harcourt, Brace and World, 1935.

Kligman, Gail. "Reclaiming the Public: A Reflection on Creating Civil Society in Romania." *East European Politics and Societies* 4 (1990): 393–438.

Kornhauser, William. *The Politics of Mass Society*. Glencoe, Ill.: Free Press of Glencoe, 1959.

de Lamartine, Alphonse. *History of the French Revolution of 1848*, 2 vols. Translated by Francis A. Durivage and William S. Chase. Boston: Phillips, Sampson and Co., 1851.

Lash, Scott, and John Urry. *The End of Organized Capitalism*. Madison, Wis.: University of Wisconsin Press, 1987.

Le Bon, Gustave. *The Psychology of Peoples*. New York: G. E. Stechert, 1912.

———. *The Psychology of Socialism*. New York: Macmillan, 1899.

———. *The Crowd: A Study of the Popular Mind*. London: T. Fisher Unwin, 1896.

Lederer, Emil. *State of the Masses*. New York: W. W. Norton, 1940.

Leeden, Michael A. "The Evolution of Italian Fascist Antisemitism." *Jewish Social Studies* 37 (1975): 3–17.

Lefebvre, Georges. *The Great Fear of 1789: Rural Panic in Revolutionary France*, translated by Joan White. London: New Left Books 1973.

Lenin, Vladimir. "The State and Revolution." In *V. I. Lenin Collected Works*, vol. 25. Moscow: Progress Publishers, 1964.

Leo XIII. *"Rerum Novarum."* In *The Papal Encyclicals in their Historical Context*, edited by Anne Fremantle. New York: Mentor-Omega Books, 1963, pp. 166–95.

Lombroso, Cesare. *Crime: Its Causes and Remedies*. Translated by Henry P. Horton. Boston: Little Brown, 1911.

Ludwig, Emil. *Talks with Mussolini*. Translated by Eden and Cedar Paul. Boston: Little Brown, 1933.

MacGregor, Ian. *The Enemies Within*. London: Collins, 1986.

Macpherson, Crawford B. *Democracy in Alberta*. Toronto: University of Toronto Press, 1953.

McGuire, M. "The Scab Watch Team." In *A Year of Our Lives Hatfield Main A Colliery Community in the Great Coal Strike of 1984/85.* "This book has been produced by the people of Hatfield Main Colliery," edited by David John Douglas. Hooligan Press, 1986.

Madden, Paul. "Some Social Characteristics of Early Nazi Party Members, 1919–1923." *Central European History* 15 (1982): 34–56.

de Man, Hendrik. *A Documentary Study of Hendrik de Man, Socialist Critic of Marxism*, edited by Peter Dodge. Princeton: Princeton University Press, 1979.

Mannheim, Karl. *Ideology and Utopia*, translated by Louis Wirth and Edward Shils. New York: Harcourt, Brace and World, 1936.

Martin, Everett Dean. *The Behavior of Crowds*. New York: Harper and Brothers, 1920.

Marx, Karl. "The Civil War in France" (First Draft, Second Draft and Address of the General Council). In *Karl Marx Friedrich Engels Gesamtausgabe*, vol. 1, part 22. Berlin: Dietz Verlag, 1978.

———. *The Class Struggles in France (1848–1850)*. New York: International Publishers, 1968.

———. *Capital*, vol. 1. Chicago: Charles Kerr, 1912.

Marx, Karl, and Frederick Engels. *Karl Marx Frederick Engels Collected Works*, 50 vols. New York: International Publishers, 1975.

———. *The Communist Manifesto*. Harmondsworth, Britain: Penguin, 1967.

Mastnak, Tomaz. "No Rationale for the Survival of Yugoslavia?" *East European Reporter* 3 (1989): 46–48.

de Maupassant, Guy. *Afloat*, translated by Laura Ensor. London: George Routledge and Sons, 1889.

Meiksens Wood, Ellen. "The Myth of the Idle Mob." In *Peasant-Citizen and Slave: The Foundations of Athenian Democracy*, pp. 5–41. London: Verso, 1988.

Michelet, Jules. *History of the French Revolution*, translated by Charles Cocks, edited by Gordon Wright. Chicago: University of Chicago, 1967.

Middlemas, Keith. *Politics in Industrial Society: The Experience of the British System since 1911*. London: Andre Deutsch, 1979.

Miliband, Ralph. *Marxism and Politics*. Oxford: Oxford University Press, 1977.

More, Thomas. *Utopia*, translated by Paul Turner. Harmondsworth, Britain: Penguin Books, 1961.

———. *Utopia*, translated by Ralph Robinson, edited by Edward Arbor. London: Edward Arbor, 1869.

Mosley, Oswald. *Tomorrow We Live*, 6th ed. London: Greater Britain Publications, 1939.

———. *Fascism: 100 Questions*. London: British Union of Fascists, 1936.

———. *The Greater Britain*. London: British Union of Fascists, 1934.

Muhlberger, Detlef. "Germany." In *The Social Basis of European Fascist Movements*, edited by Detlef Muhlberger, pp. 40–139. London: Croom Helm, 1987.

Munson, Gorham. *Aladdin's Lamp*. New York: Creative Age Press, 1945.

Mussolini, Benito. *Fascism Doctrine and Institutions*. Araita: Rome, 1935.

———. *My Autobiography*. New York: Charles Scribner's Sons, 1928.

National Union of Mineworkers. *Press Releases*. 26 January 1984, 19 February 1984, 6 March 1984.

Neumann, Sigmund. *Permanent Revolution*. New York: Frederick Praeger, 1965.

Nietzsche, Friedrich. *The Will to Power*, translated by Walter Kaufmann and R. J. Hollingdale. New York: Random House, 1968.

———. The Genealogy of Morals, translated by Horace B. Samuel. New York: Russell and Russell, 1964.

Nolte, Ernst. *Three Faces of Fascism*, translated by Leila Vennewitz. New York: Holt, Rinehart and Winston, 1966.

North Yorkshire Women Against Pit Closures. *Strike 84–85*. Leeds: 1985.

Nye, Robert A. *The Origins of Crowd Psychology: Gustave LeBon and the Crisis of Mass Democracy in the Third Republic*. London: Sage, 1975.

Oddo, Gilbert. *Slovakia and Its People*. New York: Robert Speller and Sons, 1960.

O'Duffy, Eimar. *Asses in Clover*. London: Putnam, 1933.

Ottey, Roy. *The Strike: An Insider's Story*. London: Sidgwick and Jackson, 1985.

Overy, R. J. *The Nazi Economic Recovery 1932–1938*. London: Macmillan, 1982.

Paine, Thomas. *The Rights of Man*. London: J. M. Dent, 1915.

Park, Robert E. *The Crowd and the Public*, translated by Charlotte Elsner. Chicago: University of Chicago, 1972.

Pataud, Emile, and Emile Pouget. *Syndicalism and the Co-operative Common-*

wealth (How We Shall Bring about the Revolution). Oxford: New International Publishing Co., 1913.

Payne, Stanley G. *Falange: A History of Spanish Fascism*. Stanford, Calif.: Stanford University Press, 1961.

The People of Thurcroft. *Thurcroft: A Village and the Miners' Strike*. Copyright Peter Gibbon and David Steyne. London: Spokesman, 1986.

Picard, Edmond. *L'Aryano-Sémitisme*. Brussels: Paul Lacomblez, 1898.

Plato. *The Republic*, translated by Raymond Larson. Arlington Heights, Ill.: Harlan Davidson, 1979.

"Poland: The Kaczynski Card." *East European Newsletter*, 7 April 1991, pp. 5–7.

Polonsky, Antony. *The Little Dictators*. London: Routledge and Kegan Paul, 1975.

Poulantzas, Nicos. *Political Power and Social Classes*. Translated by Timothy O'Hagan et al. London: New Left Books, 1973.

Poulson, Henning. "The Nordic States." In *The Social Basis of European Fascist Movements*, edited by Detlef Muhlberger. London: Croom Helm, 1987, pp. 155–89.

Price, Roger. *The French Second Republic: A Social History*. Ithaca, N.Y.: Cornell University Press, 1985.

Rawnsley, Stuart. "The Membership of the British Union of Fascists." In *British Fascism*, edited by Kenneth Lunn and Richard C. Thurlow, pp. 150–66. London: Croom Helm, 1980.

Revelli, Marco. "Italy." Translated by Roger Griffin. In *The Social Basis of European Fascist Movements*, edited by Detlef Muhlberger, pp. 1–39. London: Croom Helm, 1987.

Rohrich, Wilfried. "George Sorel and the Myth of Violence." In *Social Protest, Violence and Terror in Nineteenth- and Twentieth-Century Europe*, edited by Wolfgang J. Mommsen and Gerhard Hirschfeld, pp. 246–56. London: Macmillan, 1982.

Roth, Jack J. *The Cult of Violence: Sorel and the Sorelians*. Berkeley: University of California Press, 1980.

Rothschild, Joseph. *East Central Europe between the Two World Wars*. Vol. 9 of *A History of East Central Europe*, edited by Peter F. Sugar and Donald W. Treadgold. Seattle: University of Washington Press, 1974.

Rousseau, Jean-Jacques. *The Social Contract*, translated by G.D.H. Cole. London: J. M. Dent, 1973.

Rude, George. *Ideology and Popular Protest*. New York: Pantheon Books, 1980.

———. *The Crowd in History: A Study of Popular Disturbances in France and England 1730–1848*. New York: John Wiley and Sons, 1964.

———. "The London 'Mob' of the Eighteenth Century." *Historical Journal* 2 (1959): 1–18.

———. *The Crowd in the French Revolution*. Oxford: Clarendon Press, 1959.

Salazar, Oliveira. *Salazar Prime Minister of Portugal Says* . . . . Lisbon: SPN Books, n.d.

Samuel, Raphael et al. *The Enemy Within: Pit Villages and the Miner's Strike of 1984–5*. London: Routledge and Kegan Paul, 1986.

Sartori, Giovanni. "Politics Ideology and Belief Systems." *American Political Science Review* 63 (1969): 398–411.

Saville, John. "An Open Conspiracy: Conservative Politics and the Miners' Strike 1984–5." In *The Socialist Register 1985/86*, edited by Ralph Miliband et al., pp. 295–329. London: Merlin, 1986.

Scargill, Arthur. "Full Weight of State Will Not Defeat Us." *The Miner*, special issue, 30 June, 1984, p. 4.

———. "The New Unionism." *New Left Review* 92 (July–August 1975): 3–33.

Schmitter, Philippe C. "Modes of Interest Intermediation and Models of Societal Change in Western Europe." In *Trends Toward Corporatist Intermediation*, edited by P. C. Schmitter and Gerhard Lembruch, pp. 63–94. Beverly Hills, Calif.: Sage, 1979.

———. "Still the Century of Corporatism?" *Review of Politics* 36 (1974): 85–131.

Schumpeter, Joseph. *Capitalism, Socialism and Democracy*. New York: Harper and Row, 1950.

"Security Forces Storm Protesters in East Germany." *New York Times*, 9 October 1989, p. A6.

Sighele, Scipio. *La Foule criminelle: essai de psychologie collective*. Paris: Felix Alcan, 1901.

———. *Psychologie des sectes*, translated by Louis Brandin. Paris: V. Giard and E. Brière, 1898.

Silberner, Edmund. "Two Studies on Modern Anti-Semitism." *Historia Judaica* 14 (1952): 93–118.

Smith, Billy. "Nottingham/1984—Scabs—1985." *Durham Striker*. Reproduced in *The Nottinghamshire Miner* (September 1985).

Sorel, Georges. *Reflections on Violence*, translated by T. E. Hulme. London: George Allen and Unwin, 1915.

Soucy, Robert. *Fascism in France: The Case of Maurice Barrès*. Berkeley: University of California Press, 1972.

Stead, Jan. *Never the Same Again: Women and the Miners' Strike 1984–85*. London: Women's Press, 1987.

Stedman Jones, Gareth. *Outcast London*. Oxford: Clarendon Press, 1971.

Stein, Alfred. "Adolf Hitler und Gustave Le Bon." *Geschichte in Wissenschaft und Unterricht* 6 (1955): 362–68.

Sterling, Eleonore O. "Anti-Jewish Riot in Germany in 1819." *Historia Judaica* 12 (1950): 105–42.

Sternhell, Zeev. "Irrationalism and Violence in the French Radical Right: The Case of Maurice Barrès." In *Violence and Aggression in the History of Ideas*, edited by Philip P. Wiener and John Fisher, pp. 79–98. New Brunswick, N.J.: Rutgers University Press, 1974.

Sugar, Peter F., and Ivo J. Lederer, eds. *Nationalism in Eastern Europe*. Seattle: University of Washington Press, 1969.

Sutherland, Lucy. "The City of London in Eighteenth-Century Politics." In *Essays Presented to Sir Lewis Namier*, edited by Richard Pares and A.J.P. Taylor. London: Macmillan, 1956.

Taine, Hippolyte Adolphe. *The Origins of Contemporary France, The Ancient Regime*, translated by John Durand. New York: Henry Holt and Co., 1896.

———. *The Origins of Contemporary France, The French Revolution*, 2 vols., translated by John Durand. New York: Henry Holt and Co., 1896.

Talmon, J. L. *Political Messianism*. New York: Frederick Praeger, 1960.

Tarde, Gabriel. *Penal Philosophy*, translated by Rapelje Howell. Boston: Little Brown, 1912.

———. *L'Opinion et la foule*. Paris: Felix Alcan, 1904.

———. *The Laws of Imitation*, translated by Elsie Clews Parsons. London: Henry Holt, 1903.

Taylor, Jack et al. "Breakaways Merely Weaken Our Common Strength—Area Officials." *Yorkshire Miner* 81 (August 1985): 1.

Thalheimer, August. "On Fascism," translated by Judy Joseph. *Telos* 40 (Summer 1979): 109–22.

Thompson, Edward P. "The Moral Economy of the English Crowd in the Eighteenth Century." *Past and Present* 50 (February 1971): 76–136.

———. *The Making of the English Working Class*. New York: Random House, 1964.

Thompson, William. *Labor Rewarded*. "By one of the Idle Classes." London: Hunt and Clarke, 1827.

———. *An Inquiry into the Principles of Distribution of Wealth Most Conducive to Human Happiness: Applied to the Newly proposed System of Voluntary Equality of Wealth*. London: Longman, 1824.

Tilly, Charles, and Lynn H. Lees. "The People of June 1848." In *Revolution and Reaction*, edited by Roger Price, pp. 170–209. New York: Harper and Row, 1975.

"The Timisoara Proclamation." *East European Reporter* 4 (1990): 32–35.

Tint, Herbert. *France Since 1918*. New York: St. Martin's Press, 1980.

Traugott, Mark. *Armies of the Poor: Determinants of Working-Class Participation in the Parisian Insurrection of June 1848*. Princeton: Princeton University Press, 1985.

Traynor, Ian. "Romania Warns Off Street Protesters." *Guardian* (London). 20 February 1990, p. 8.

Trotsky, Leon. *The Struggle Against Fascism in Germany*. New York: Pathfinder Press, 1971.

de Viel Castel, Count Horace. *Memoirs of Count Horace de Viel Castel*, translated by Charles Bousfield. London: Remington, 1888.

Volney, C. F. *The Ruins*. New York: Peter Eckler, 1890.

Walter, Richard D. "What Became of the Degenerate?" *Journal of the History of Medicine and Allied Sciences* 11 (October 1956): 422–29.

Watson, William. *A Decacordon of Ten Quodlibeticall Questions Concerning Religion and State*. 1602. Reprinted as a facsimile in D. M. Rogers, ed., *English Recusant Literature 1558–1640*, vol. 197. Ilkely, England: Scholar Press, 1974.

Weber, Max. *The Protestant Ethic and the Spirit of Capitalism*, translated by Talcott Parsons. New York: Charles Scribner's Sons, 1958.

―――. " 'Objectivity' in Social Science and Social Policy." In *Max Weber on the Methodology of the Social Sciences*, edited by Edward Shils and Henry Finch. Glencoe, Ill.: Free Press, 1949.

"What Arthur Scargill Thinks of You." *Nottinghamshire Miner* 1 (February 1985).

Williams, Raymond. *Keywords*. London: Fontana, 1976.

―――. *Culture and Society, 1750–1950*. New York: Harper and Row, 1958.

Winterton, Jonathon, and Ruth Winterton. *Coal, Crisis and Conflict*. Manchester, England: Manchester University Press, 1989.

Wood, Allen, W. *Hegel's Ethical Thought*. Cambridge: Cambridge University Press, 1990.

Zola, Emile. *Germinal*. Edited by Ernest Alfred Vizetelly. London: Chatto and Windus, 1901.

Index

About the Author

PETER HAYES is a temporary Assistant Professor of Political Science at Iowa State University. A British citizen, he earned his Ph.D. at the University of Illinois at Urbana-Champaign.